Praise for *Transformational Speaking*

"Gail Larsen's wise book will help anyone tap into the remarkable power of story, transforming not just the listener but the storyteller as well. In our changing world, with unprecedented possibilities for communicating, these lessons are vital."

—**Larry Dossey**, MD, author of *The Extraordinary Power of Ordinary Things*

"Gail's method is a remarkably powerful way to build leadership skills that effectively integrates inner healing and transformation with practical skill building. I cannot recommend her book or her work more highly, as they have been truly transformative for me and improved my speaking skills immeasurably."

—**Nina Simons**, co-executive director, Bioneers

"Whether the subject is bookkeeping, paleontology, God, or personal transformation, there is nothing more moving, inspiring, or effective than speaking from your heart. Gail Larsen will take you there."

—**Lindsay Wagner**, actress, producer, humanitarian

"We all want to be part of a bigger story, something beyond ourselves that allows us to serve the common good and find personal fulfillment. Gail Larsen uniquely helps you down the path of finding that story in yourself and communicating it to others. I can think of no greater gift than what Gail offers each and every reader."

—**Dr. Mark Albion**, cofounder, Net Impact, and author of the *New York Times* best seller *Making a Life, Making a Living* and *True to Yourself*

"Brilliant! Our stories can make a real and human contact like nothing else, and the time to tell our stories is now. Gail's message, backed by decades of experience and a sound method, is clear: Be the one to set in motion the world-transforming story that your life, and your life alone, has prepared you to tell."

—**Sankara Saranam**, author of *God Without Religion*

"In this powerful and insightful book, Gail touches the Source, both of our own humanity and of our capacity to speak our truths in ways which touch the humanity and the hearts of others. By embracing the guidance and wisdom on these pages, transformational speakers have the opportunity to ignite transformational conversations— those that can help shape life-affirming futures in our organizations, our communities, and on this fragile and beautiful planet. BRAVO!"

—**Juanita Brown**, PhD, cofounder, The World Café

"Gail Larsen is a master teacher who is catalyzing the emergence of a sustainable world through Real Speaking. Now her book brings this powerful approach alive on the page. Anyone who wants to speak out and make a difference in the world will benefit from reading *Transformational Speaking*."

—**Peggy Taylor and Rick Ingrasci**, MD, coauthors of *Chop Wood, Carry Water: A Guide to Finding Spiritual Fulfillment in Everyday Life*

"Gail Larsen is an exceptional storyteller, practitioner, and entrepreneur who embodies the title of her new book. She *is* changing the world with her unique gifts and talents. Some books offer lessons and others inspiration, but few accomplish both while providing hands-on practical tools and advice. Keep *Transformational Speaking* handy—you're going to use it for years to come."

—**Pam Chaloult**, chief operating officer, Renewal Partners/ Endswell Foundation, and former co-executive director, Social Venture Network

"Gail's thoughtful and practical application of indigenous wisdom to those who address today's contemporary audiences allows them to create greater impact and meaning by accessing their authentic power. Using the time-tested effect of story, those who apply the principles of *Transformational Speaking* will penetrate differences and resistance and be heard. This wonderful book provides a lens into speaking that is not taught elsewhere. It will transform your experience as a public speaker."

—**Richard C. Whiteley**, cofounder, The Forum Corporation, and author of *The Customer Driven Company* and *Customer Centered Growth*

"While I had been a speaker for years before taking Real Speaking, I had never heard: 'You are a wonderful and compelling speaker. I love hearing you speak.' Working with Gail transformed my whole experience of speaking from enduring it to really enjoying it. Now the teachings from Gail's workshop are available to you in this excellent book. *Transformational Speaking* is must reading for anyone who does any speaking."

—**Margaret Paul**, PhD, coauthor of *Do I Have to Give Up Me to Be Loved By You?*

"*Transformational Speaking* is an invaluable resource and practical guide for anyone, at any age, in any profession, to become more skilled and effective in all aspects of how to communicate in compelling and authentic ways."

—**Angeles Arrien**, PhD, cultural anthropologist and author of *The Four-Fold Way* and *The Second Half of Life*

"If you buy only one book on speaking, let this be the one! With decades of high-level experience, Gail Larsen is a true master in engaging the authentic voice of every speaker. *Transformational Speaking* will help you be more effective in any speaking situation, as you learn to speak from what Gail calls your 'home zone,' that place of integrity, depth and power."

—**Dr. Brian Nattrass**, Batten Fellow of the Darden Graduate School of Business; managing partner, Sustainability Partners, Inc.; and coauthor of *Dancing with the Tiger* and *The Natural Step for Business*

"Wise and accessible, *Transformational Speaking* will help you leap forward in your confidence and understanding with practical tools and a framework to support your unique voice. Gail Larsen's work is having a significant impact on the ability of social change leaders to communicate their messages to inspire support and action. This timely book makes her excellent training available to anyone who has something to say and wants to speak with power and confidence."

—**Joel Solomon**, president, Renewal Partners; executive director, Endswell Foundation; and board chair, Hollyhock Retreat Centre

"Gail Larsen has taken her place as a master teacher, showing us how to use the gift of story to inspire and teach people to be a transformative force through speaking. This is an invaluable resource for people of all professions."

—**Sandra Ingerman**, author of *Soul Retrieval*
and *How to Heal Toxic Thoughts*

"Gail Larsen shows you how to speak from the heart—the only place from which you can really reach an audience. This is the best book on public speaking I've read."

—**W. Brian Arthur**, economist and keynote speaker

"Refreshing and original, *Transformational Speaking* will help you celebrate your inherent gifts and values, and speak with clarity, conviction, and confidence. Gail leads you step by step to find your voice and be heard."

—**Wally Amos**, inspirational speaker, author, and cookie man

"This inspiring book approaches public speaking from the core outward, connecting us with the passionate voice that lies behind our deeper life's purpose. I find myself returning again and again to the wisdom in these pages."

—**Chris Jordan**, photographic artist

"*Transformational Speaking* presents a spiritual path in a how-to book—what a rare find! It's beautifully written, passionate, and totally authentic. Gail is someone you WANT to learn from, and she has so much to share. Her teaching is filled with depth and presence and makes you realize that a podium is a meditation cushion in disguise. And vice versa, too. Become a better speaker, Gail's way, and you're bound to find more than a little enlightenment along the way.

—**Raphael Cushnir**, author of *The One Thing Holding You Back:*
Unleashing the Power of Emotional Connection

Transformational

SPEAKING

Tell me a fact and I'll listen.
Tell me a truth and I'll learn.
But tell me a story,
And it will live in my heart forever.

—NATIVE AMERICAN WISDOM

Transformational

SPEAKING

If You Want to Change the World,
Tell a Better Story

GAIL LARSEN

CELESTIAL ARTS
Berkeley | Toronto

Celestial Arts
an imprint of Ten Speed Press
PO Box 7123
Berkeley, California 94707
www.tenspeed.com

Distributed in Australia by Simon and Schuster Australia, in Canada by Ten Speed Press Canada, in New Zealand by Southern Publishers Group, in South Africa by Real Books, and in the United Kingdom and Europe by Publishers Group UK.

Cover design by The BookDesigners
Text design by BookMatters, Berkeley

Previously published as *Transformational Speaking* (iUniverse, 2007; 978-0-59547-991-7).

Library of Congress Cataloging-in-Publication Data
Larsen, Gail.
  Transformational speaking : if you want to change the world, tell a better story /
By Gail Larsen.
      p.   cm.
  Includes bibliographical references and index.
  Summary: "A guide to public speaking written for presenters seeking to be agents of change, whether in a business or in their community"—Provided by publisher.
  ISBN 978-1-58761-342-5
  1. Public speaking. I. Title.
  PN4129.15.L37   2009
  808.5'1—dc22   2008038885

Printed in the United States of America

First printing, 2009
1 2 3 4 5 6 7 8 9 10 — 13 12 11 10 09

With love and gratitude to
Angeles Arrien,
who brought the loving world of Spirit alive to me
and accepts nothing less than we claim the power
and magnificence of our Original Medicine,

and

President Barack Obama,
whose words and presence have ignited a new story
and demonstrated to the world the power of
transformational speaking

Contents

Preface   xii

Acknowledgments   xv

Introduction: The Principles
of Transformational Speaking   1

PART 1   THE **HEART** OF
TRANSFORMATIONAL SPEAKING

Honoring Your Original Medicine

1   Public Speaking Transformed
*Displacing Prevailing Myths
with Enduring Principles*   9

2   Be Yourself—Everyone Else Is Taken
Claiming Your Gifts and Talents   23

3   God Said, "Ha!"
*Finding the Speech You
Were Born to Give*   36

4   From Comfort Zone to Home Zone™
*Expressing the New Edge®
of Emotional Connection*   45

PART 2   THE **ART** OF
TRANSFORMATIONAL SPEAKING

**Connecting with Your Audience
to Catalyze Change**

5   Truth Well Spoken
*Mastering the Four Disciplines
of Star Quality*   63

6 Know Thyself, Then Thy Audience
Preparing to Be Surprised 78

7 Look, Ma—No Script!
Crafting a Masterful Presentation 89

8 Show Time!
Taking the Stage 106

PART 3   THE **ENERGETICS** OF
TRANSFORMATIONAL SPEAKING
Remaining Whole in the Work of Change

9 Body Rules
Extreme Cherishment of Your Precious,
Worthy Self 121

10 Energy Awareness
Understanding and Managing
Invisible Dynamics 129

11 The Alchemy of Change
Choosing Power over Force 143

12 Tell a Better Story
Inspiring the Impossible 153

Resources
Written Communications to Support
a Professional Presentation 167

Bibliography 179

Index 181

About the Author 189

Permissions 190

Preface

Everyone—including you—has the capacity to deliver a powerful and inspiring message when they go deep enough to find what is theirs to say. I begin with my story so you will know why I, a person who has suffered from a deep-seated fear of public speaking and would have preferred never to make a speech, might be just the person to support you in giving voice to what matters most to you.

I did not come to speaking with joy or ease. But life was unwilling to allow me to stay seated. To the contrary, I would have to stand up in a way I never dreamed I was capable of. I would have to speak out over and over in front of large groups of people. In time, I discovered that dealing with fear was only half the battle. Once I developed a modicum of confidence, I had to learn to go beyond my comfort zone to become the speaker I was born to be.

In 1981, I received an early-morning telegram from the president of the United States congratulating me on receiving the U.S. Small Business Administration Tennessee Small Businessman of the Year award and inviting me to the White House. The visibility and success of my Tennessee Women's Career Conventions had led to my nomination—in fact, my first such convention had been the occasion of my first speech, to four thousand people! But I had no idea of the magnitude of the honor I was to receive, nor the number of speaking invitations that would come my way as the first woman to be the small business "man" of the year in my state.

And so I began the arduous job of developing a skill that so far had eluded me. Television appearances and radio interviews were an effortless extension of my ease in connecting one on one with people, but when it came to addressing a large group, I had no clue how to get good at what was being asked of me. Before every speaking engagement, I would spend hours writing out my speech and then deliver it verbatim, looking up at the audience as often as possible while taking care not to lose my place. I would hang on to the lectern with both hands in the hope people wouldn't see me shaking.

To learn about the art and craft of speaking, I joined the National Speakers Association (NSA), the worldwide professional organization for platform presenters. Within a few years, starstruck and intrigued by this new world of fascinating personalities and inspiring presentations, I was hired as NSA's first full-time executive vice president, selected not for my speaking abilities but for my business and management acumen. I was thrilled to be running a growing organization in its entrepreneurial phase, my speaking role confined to board meetings and welcoming members to our various workshops and conventions.

When I resigned from NSA four years later to support the voices I found most inspiring, I became a marketing strategist for a few top speakers. In 1991, I began an annual program called Keynote Camp to provide a comprehensive, intensive introduction to professional speaking.

In 2000, events converged to cause me to bring my work as a speaker and trainer to center stage. It was a time of painful endings, including the deaths of both my parents as well as the dissolution of a business venture in which I had invested three years of love and visionary energy. In profound grief, I needed to do something "small," manageable. Keynote Camp, previously a sideline, became my sole professional focus, renamed Real Speaking®. Around the same time, I penned *Madame Ovary: Midlife as an Art*

Form, a humorous chronicle of the trauma of my midlife years, written as a tribute to my dad, who loved my stories. Publishing that little book and presenting "the Madame" on stage opened the door to applying my years of background in professional speaking to becoming the Real Speaker I wanted to be.

Speaking suddenly became *fun*. I was sharing something vitally important to me in a way that expressed my eclectic personality, talking from my heart about the full range of my life journey and applying it to the challenges of women and men alike as we navigate our middle years. Life had stripped me of my façade of invincibility, replacing it with a vulnerability that allowed me to connect more deeply with others. Together, my audiences and I were laughing and crying and learning about and celebrating the beauty of who we are when we express ourselves authentically. My decades of experience in formulating, marketing, and delivering speeches had magically come together in a program that encouraged each of us to embrace and tell our stories and be the amazing and original works of art we are here to be. Finally I had found the "secret" of speaking.

It has been said that we teach what we most need to learn. Over the years, as witness and guide to the intimate and life-changing work of Real Speaking, I've seen countless people break through what stops them and express the freedom that comes from speaking out in an authentic and original voice. This book reveals the inner process and outer exercises and techniques that have worked for both my clients and me. May it inspire you to express the full range of the gift you already are and, just maybe, to step into your destiny as a transformational speaker.

Acknowledgments

Although this book reflects what I am learning from twenty-five years in the world of speaking, it came together surprisingly quickly because of the enormous support of my friends and allies. Foremost among them is Elizabeth Wolf, editor of the first edition in 2007, whose enthusiasm never waned as she talked with me for months about possible structure before she ever had a word to read. Then, when she did, she continued working with love and commitment while juggling multiple demands.

For those of us whose work lives are not devoted to writing, I now completely understand why Virginia Woolf extolled the sanctity of "a room of one's own." Peggy Taylor and Rick Ingrasci offered me their home on Whidbey Island, Washington, in July and August of 2007, providing the impetus not only to write but also to answer a soul call to both place and community. Then, once the initial draft was in Elizabeth Wolf's capable hands, I was offered a fellowship at Hedgebrook, a writing retreat on Whidbey Island for "women authoring change," to complete the manuscript. How could one not be inspired in a private cabin in the woods with healthy meals and lavish comfort food? My deep thanks to Amy Wheeler and Vito Zingarelli of Hedgebrook for seeing the promise of this book and providing a room of my own to complete it, and to Hedgebrook founder Nancy Nordhoff and the many donors who make this haven available to women writers.

When Elizabeth suggested a fresh look would be valuable, Linda Solomon stepped in to provide her penetrating insight and editing skill. Her frequent notes "I love this!" or "This one page is worth the price of the book!" were as welcome as her challenging questions. (Actually, more so, but it was all good.) Thank you, Linda, for not letting me get away with anything that wasn't absolutely clear to you and for asking for even more stories, stories, stories!

My dear friend Runa Bouius suggested I spend time writing instead of accepting speaking engagements that didn't make my heart sing. Ellen Kleiner of Blessingway Authors' Services has been a wealth of wisdom, lovingly dispensed. She also submitted the first edition for the 2008 Indie Book Awards where it was a finalist in the "how-to" category. The first edition was also a finalist in the self-help/motivational category of the National Best Books 2008 Awards sponsored by USABookNews.com.

Ariella Tilsen helped me blast through writer's block by suggesting I write three pages a day, even if they were "really crappy pages, double spaced, in large type." Sandy Miller generously made the time to proofread because she wanted to be the first to read the book. Susan Hyatt has cheered me on in our weekly phone conversations devoted to supporting each other's dreams.

Offering my programs at Hollyhock Retreat Centre and Social Venture Network has introduced me to a world of visionary messengers who catalyze both personal and planetary change. My heartfelt thanks to Pam Chaloult, Deb Nelson, Carol Newell, Joel Solomon, Dana Bass Solomon, Karen Mahon, Julia Watson, and Clare Day.

The work of many people informs my approach. Those who have studied with Angeles Arrien will recognize her influence. Jeri Burgdorf introduced me to the concept of the enhanced level of speaking I call the "home zone." As I constantly read, attend speeches, and collect ideas, I may have inadvertently referenced your work without attribution; if so, please accept my apology and let me know so I may credit you in the next edition.

The challenging times in which we live motivated me to get the first edition out quickly, using the publishing services of iUniverse. At the same time, literary agent Jeff Herman began his representation, and now I have the joy of working with Ten Speed Press/ Celestial Arts. My heartfelt thanks to a creative publishing house and to Aaron Wehner, who walked me through my many questions to be sure we would be a good team in bringing *Transformational Speaking* to a larger audience. My editor, Genoveva Llosa, an "advocate for the reader," asked clarifying questions and offered suggestions that resulted in an even stronger book.

My clients, my teachers, and my friends expand my horizons and are a constant source of inspiration and delight. Because of them, I get a front-row seat for the stories that are transforming the world, one audience at a time. I am grateful . . . beyond words.

The Principles of Transformational Speaking

Are you a change agent? Do you see a situation that needs to be transformed and have something to say about it? Perhaps you offer an essential service or an inventive solution that helps people address challenge and transition. You may be a visionary leader of an organization catalyzing social or environmental change, or a healer who supports others through health or spiritual crises. Perhaps you have written a book you know in your heart can make a significant difference or created impressive works of art or music that deserve a wider audience. You could be a far-seeing business-person or a spiritual elder or a concerned citizen with thoughtful ideas or a passion for your organization, your community, or your world. Whatever it is that commands your attention, you want your words to matter. And you know that by becoming a great speaker, your voice will be heard.

The question, of course, is how? This book offers the liberating and proven method I have been offering my clients through Real Speaking workshops and coaching since 1991. It has evolved through the synthesis and integration of my own journey of speaking and the personal work in which I have engaged to live with a sense of meaning and genuine self-expression. Real Speaking has supported countless people of purpose in speaking publicly, with passion and ease, about what matters most to them. In the

1

following pages, I'll show you the way to inspire transformational change through your own spoken word.

As an executive vice president of the worldwide National Speakers Association in the mid-1980s and an admitted "speaker junkie," I've seen literally thousands of presenters in action. There are two kinds of memorable speakers. There are those who impress us with their delivery and style and cause us to say, "He was a great speaker!"—then return to our lives and our work unchanged. Sure, these speakers may give a great performance and even get a standing ovation, but it's akin to a rock concert where we see a favorite act, work ourselves into fervor, and then go home to life as usual.

Then there are those who arouse us on an inner level, awakening us to what we care about and prompting serious inquiry about the changes we're committed to making. That's transformational speaking, and it's rare indeed. The best speakers aren't "canned," predictable, or practiced students of technique. They come to their craft in their own inimitable way. They celebrate who they are and bring the essence of their true selves forward. They touch our hearts. Their speaking is not a performance; it is uncommon self-expression. It's not only professional but also human. And we leave changed by being there, knowing that what we experienced is *real.*

Transformational speakers shape-shift what people believe is possible. They address real issues without fear or apology. They are catalysts for transforming lives. They alter the course of events by inspiring others to take an action that ripples through their circles of influence. They plant seeds of needed change that will impact the future of individuals, families, workplaces, communities, nations, and our sacred earth.

Anyone who is committed to becoming a true agent of change can become a transformational speaker. If you want to spread the word of what matters to you to an audience, becoming a transformational speaker will allow you to inspire others, influence what people believe and do, and alter events. But you can't get there with tired techniques and scripting that obscure your deep caring and capacity to inspire.

In today's climate of distrust of much of our leadership, speakers who are perfectly rehearsed and claim to have the answers cause us to be very suspicious indeed. In politics, such speakers have made promises they haven't kept. In companies, they have delivered flavors of the month with flair, proposing systems change that fades into oblivion almost overnight. In the nonprofit world, they have prompted us to wonder how this organization is different from hundreds of others and whether the requested donation will become a breaking-news scandal. In personal growth or health, they tell us something we've already heard and tried to no avail. Our challenging times call for communicators who aren't slick or superficial and don't pretend to know all the answers to the question of how to create a world that works. Instead, we need people who are passionately committed to healthy people, healthy communities, and a healthy planet to inspire meaningful dialogue and real action.

Such change artists are everywhere. Paul Hawken's best-selling book *Blessed Unrest* identifies "a worldwide grassroots movement of hope and humanity" comprising more than one million organizations and untold numbers of engaged citizens passionately committed to creating a new story about human life on planet Earth. To create that better story, the most important voice to hear is your own so you can energetically engage in what calls to you. Then you can't help but speak up and out, because you are stepping into your destiny work in this vast movement for "hope and humanity."

Transformational Speaking is written expressly for speakers and would-be speakers involved in this global groundswell with no name, change agents and visionary messengers from all walks of life who wish to use their voices in the service of change. You don't have to be a Susan B. Anthony or a Martin Luther King Jr. to speak out. If you're tired of the old story and long to tell a better one that uplifts both you and others, then *Transformational Speaking* will show you how to do just that.

Recently I had a conversation with journalist and women's rights advocate Gloria Steinem, who inspired enormous social change by committing herself to a new story that would make the world better for all because it honored women. As we talked about public speaking, she said she began speaking because she had to. The opportunities were there to reach people in a way her writing did not. She allowed, too, that she still gets nervous and her mouth goes dry when she gets up to speak. Surprised, I asked, "What do you think that's about?" She replied, "It's like malaria; you recover but the fever keeps coming back. It happens to me when the stakes are high."

Today the stakes are high. It is time for many voices to be heard. This is not the moment of singular heroes so much as it is a time for many to take single heroic actions. By telling a better story—a transformational story that awakens others to new possibilities— you plant seeds of change. The transformational story comes from deep within you and reflects what you most care about. Although people can and will argue with your interpretation of the facts, no one can argue with the truth of your experience, making a well-told story the most effective tool for persuasion. You know it is taking wing in those moments when your audience is completely silent as they track every word, when the applause is sustained, and especially when you hear later that what you said and the way you said it inspired change.

Transformational speaking recognizes that we are all originals, nowhere else duplicated. This is an indigenous teaching—that we are all "original medicine," born to this earth with gifts and talents that are ours and ours alone. If we do not bring those gifts and talents forward, they are lost to the world for all time. Yet in a society that teaches conformity, finding the part of ourselves able and willing to stand out can be a stretch.

And so it goes with speaking. You can learn techniques to alleviate anxiety and practice skills that get you through a presentation with some degree of comfort. Or you can go on an inner journey to find what you really have to say and your singular way of saying it. You mine the deep well of your life experience and give voice to what has heart and meaning for you. You do it your way because you are an original, and only then do you work with techniques to refine your skills and meet people where they are. Then you can stand out. And inherent in standing out is facing your fears of being seen for who you are, what you love, and the position you are taking on what really matters to you.

Speaking techniques, applied prematurely, will only distance you from your greatness and from the best you have to give an audience. So I urge you to give up the notion that becoming a great speaker is about learning techniques to "fix" how you speak and instead join me in an adventure that takes you to the discovery of what is yours and yours alone to say.

The following six principles, expanded upon in chapter 1 and reinforced throughout this book, comprise the foundation for becoming a transformational speaker:

Principle #1: You are an original, nowhere else duplicated.

Principle #2: You are a hero on a journey, and your journey defines your message.

Principle #3: The world we experience, both personal and planetary, reflects and expresses who we are individually and collectively.

Principle #4: You can't figure it all out, you can't make anything happen, and you can't make anyone do anything. Every one of us holds a different strand of the web of life and we each must heed our own call.

Principle #5: Use your authentic power with those who can hear you rather than the force of argument with those who can't.

Principle #6: You must be personally sustainable to do the work of change. Cherish your precious, worthy self.

In the following pages, we first journey to the *heart* of speaking, finding, honoring, and cultivating our original medicine. Next we'll learn more about the *art* of speaking as we discover how to meet audience members where they are with a masterful presentation. Finally we'll explore the *energetics* of speaking, which includes personal sustainability and the emerging arena of energy management. The resource section at the end of the book contains practical tools to enhance your proficiency and professionalism with written communications to help you manage logistics like a pro.

Transformational Speaking invites you to consider questions you may not typically contemplate in the busyness of life. To get full value from our journey together, take the time to actively engage in the questions asked throughout the book. I urge you to dig deep to explore your values, your life experience, and what you stand for, as such inquiry is integral to the journey.

Sound like hard work? It's actually fun and liberating to open up in ways you haven't yet imagined to create connection and catalyze change. As you commit to becoming a transformational speaker, you will realize greater self-trust in all of your communications, whether you are speaking with one person or thousands. And there's no reason not to get started right now, because you have nothing to lose except preconceived notions about yourself and about speaking that keep you from powerfully expressing yourself in a way that will ignite real and lasting change. You have within you the capacity to be a transformational speaker and to tell a better story that can change the world.

> Whenever a feeling is voiced with truth and frankness, whenever a deed is the clear expression of sentiment, a mysterious and far-reaching influence is exerted. At first it acts on those who are inwardly receptive. But the circle grows larger and larger. The root of all influence lies in one's own inner being: given true and vigorous expression in word and deed, its effect is great. The effect is but the reflection of something that emanates from one's own heart.
>
> —From *I Ching* or *Book of Changes*

Part 1 THE **HEART** OF TRANSFORMATIONAL SPEAKING

Honoring Your Original Medicine

1

Public Speaking Transformed

Displacing Prevailing Myths with Enduring Principles

Many of us admire great speakers and see them as a rarified lot, naturally gifted with a special capacity for great communication. Without an inside knowledge of the field, it's easy to believe they stand up and the right words flow through them at any time and on any subject. Compelling communicators create an aura that causes us to proclaim them "naturals." If public speaking seems unnatural to us, we are likely to regard speaking as an exceptional talent that passed most of us by. It is time to demystify that belief along with any other myths that stand in the way of your capacity to be a transformational speaker.

For example, many years ago I heard radio personality Paul Harvey, whom I had admired for decades, speak at a professional gathering. I was mesmerized by his talk. A few months later he was on the program for another convention I was attending. I couldn't wait to hear him again, expecting another great speech. Imagine my surprise and disappointment when he delivered, word for word, the same presentation I'd heard earlier. I felt cheated!

That was before I knew the maxim of professional speaking: "It's easier to find a new audience than to develop a new speech."

Celebrity speakers have mastered the art of one great talk. Although today's speaking market considers that approach "canned," the apparent ease with which a professional speaker takes the platform belies a lot of preparation and hard work.

If we aspire to a brilliantly orchestrated performance for every communication, we set ourselves up for frustration. This ideal is not something we can or will achieve when our speaking covers a variety of situations, nor can we stick to one talk and remain current as we navigate a world of change. However, one stellar talk that communicates our core message is a great place to start, both to prove to ourselves that we can do it and to provide the foundation for stepping out and expressing ourselves wholeheartedly around what matters most. Then our presentation will change as we do. If it doesn't, we will be depending on "yesterday's masterpiece," as one of my clients eloquently dubbed his own story, rather than growing and expanding to be of greater service.

Dispelling the Myths of Great Speaking

There are countless ways to stop yourself from moving into your capacity to speak well, myths I want to dispel at the outset.

MYTH #1: *Great Speakers Feel No Fear*

The primary way most of us stop ourselves from speaking is by letting fear take over. Buddhism lists five top human fears, and "fear of speaking in front of a public assembly" is the last. The four preceding it are fear of loss of life, loss of livelihood, loss of reputation, and a supernatural event. When you consider it's possible to accomplish all five with one unfortunate speech, it's no wonder fear looms so large.

Fear is normal. Acknowledging this, many accomplished speakers have learned to transform it from enemy to ally and turn fight or flight into flow. Preparation and practice help, as does recognizing the surge of energy in your body as a signal that you're ready to "go on." The noted Gestalt psychotherapist Fritz Perls reminded us, "Fear is excitement without the breath." In this book, we will address rather than discount this fear, because for many it is so extreme that important voices are never heard.

MYTH #2: *There Is a "Right Way" to Do It*

In addition to the myth that speaking is a natural talent you either have or you don't, another is that there is "a way" to do it, a way you don't know. There is, in fact, a way—but it is not available to you when you reach for a set of techniques that only removes you from your personal magic. Applied prematurely, techniques obscure the best you have to bring forward in your speaking.

The way to become a great speaker is by drawing forth your real self. From that tender, elusive, complex place springs your best material. This process requires being willing to excavate your life experience and explore the parts of yourself you have edited and rehearsed into oblivion in order to fit in. Great speaking is about standing out, in *your* way. Niceties, platitudes, and conformity will not cut it.

MYTH #3: *You're at the Mercy of the Person Who Invited You*

Another myth is that you have no control over the speaking environment. You show up and take what you're given. Yet what is more deadly than being placed on a dais as part of a panel, hunched over a table microphone for which you have to compete when you want to speak? Or attempting to be heard over the din of a networking event where people are more interested in talking to each other than listening to you, the presenter? The professional speaker's worst nightmare is speaking after a long cocktail hour and formal dinner; except for the humorists, most won't even consider that time slot. It is perfectly acceptable—and indeed, necessary—to ask for what you want and need to bring your best to your audience. A seasoned speaker will never leave these matters to chance.

MYTH #4: *Storytelling Is the Key to Connecting with Your Audience*

This myth has a seed of truth to it. Storytelling is fundamental to your success as a speaker, but it cannot be a story contrived to support a point. It must be a real story, well told, that your audience can relate to and apply to what matters to them. Techniques proffered for connecting to an audience, such as telling jokes or making eye contact, are superficial when compared with the importance of reaching deep into your heart to find what you have to say. Going deep becomes an ongoing practice. Discovering your best stories and staying alert to the good stories that find you are primary steps in bringing you and your speaking alive. You connect with your audience only by first connecting with yourself.

MYTH #5: *Good Speaking Is Good Acting*

Many assume that good speaking is good acting. There are former actors who train speakers, as well as media coaches who provide instruction on conveying your message while concealing what you wish to keep from public view. Either can offer a valuable service at specific times in your development, but if you embrace this approach as the singular path to good speaking, you run the risk of coming across as inauthentic or evasive.

MYTH #6: *You Should Give the Audience What They Want*

Although knowing your audience and their expectations is essential to your preparation, within the audience is an unspoken hunger for something for which they have not yet found words and may not even know is possible. Henry Ford, who went beyond the limits of people's imaginations by creating the Model T Ford, said, "If I had asked people what they wanted, they would have said, 'a faster horse.'" As the speaker, you are the one who can give a voice to something felt but not yet expressed, or invite others into territory they would not otherwise explore. You arc the one who can make the unusual and unknown familiar so that people will stretch beyond their habitual boundaries.

Transformational speaking requires that you first know yourself and the message you have to deliver no matter the occasion. You cannot be a great speaker if you accept requests to talk about subjects for which you have no passion or develop material only in response to what "sells." No matter the subject or the audience, your job is to offer the essential message you are here to give. If you do not, you are unable to show up as the original you are. Absolute clarity about your message simplifies your preparation and amplifies your impact.

MYTH #7: *A Speaking Coach Can Fix You and Tell You What to Do. If Not, There's Always PowerPoint*

Considering that most coaching aims to impose techniques to fix what isn't working, it's no surprise that many experience speaking as putting forward a false front. Speaking techniques can actually prevent the discovery of what is most compelling and original about you. Great speaking is less about being "fixed" than being found. When you come home to yourself and discover your best material and unique way of communicating, you'll find there's nothing broken. Then you can develop the skills—and there are only a few of them—that will maximize your greatness. As for PowerPoint, it pales in comparison to the dynamic presentation of which you are capable as a fully expressed human being. Computer-generated visuals have become so commonplace that they will mark you as a mediocre speaker unless you use them to enhance rather than duplicate your spoken word.

Now that we have addressed—and hopefully dispelled—the prevailing myths that may be stopping you, let me expand on the principles that support you in becoming a powerful voice for change.

The Six Principles of Transformational Speaking

Before we can catalyze change through our speaking, each of us needs to cultivate a level of inner personal growth and awareness that establishes the foundation on which we build a compelling platform. The following principles contain essential understandings that will support you as a transformational speaker.

PRINCIPLE #1: *You Are an Original, Nowhere Else Duplicated*

We each have a singular set of gifts and talents that define our role in change. Indigenous cultures call our natural attributes and abilities our "original medicine." No one is more special than another, but each unique expression is essential and irreplaceable. In a society that more often encourages us to fit in rather than stand out, the process of excavating and revealing our originality is an essential step to fully experiencing and expressing our true gifts. Knowing and accepting your medicine is core to expressing your personal power, strength, and understanding.

We often are unaware of our medicine or devalue it because our inherent gifts come naturally to us. What is natural is effortless, so it can seem "ordinary." We also can obscure our medicine by pursuing directions that are not aligned with who we really are and who we are here to be.

As a speaker, it is not uncommon to wish to emulate someone you admire. I'm often told by an audience member who has heard a wonderful speaker, "I want to be just like her!" That's missing the point; the point is to be just like *you*—not the one you want to hide, but the real you yet to be revealed in your speaking.

In a famous statement often erroneously attributed to Nelson Mandela, Marianne Williamson says in *A Return to Love*, "When we are liberated from our own fear, our presence automatically liberates others." When you see speakers standing in their full power, giving it all they've got, whether or not you agree with them you know they're aligned with their essential essence. Their communication appears effortless; they neither push nor hold back. No matter how controversial the stand, you know they are at home in their own skin.

Being able to put words to your medicine provides a touchstone for your decisions, much like a purpose statement for your life. For example, my own medicine draws on courage, humor, intuitive insight, and reverence for beauty to fuel my purpose, which is to be a champion of revealing our magnificence through authentic self-expression. A client summed up my medicine as a "midwife of the soul." When you commit to make choices based on your true capacities, decisions on which audiences to serve and which to decline become easier. You can't do it all! Serve where your heart sings and your true medicine can shine and be celebrated.

PRINCIPLE #2: *You Are a Hero on a Journey,*
and Your Journey Defines Your Message

Comparative mythologist Joseph Campbell, in his legendary PBS interviews with Bill Moyers, brought into the public lexicon the "hero's journey" found in world mythologies and religions. The stories of those heroes, or archetypes, provide significant lessons that apply to life's challenges. An *archetype*, from the Greek for "original," is the model after which similar things are patterned. When you begin to understand the heroic nature of your own life journey, you'll find archetypal lessons for your speaking that can inspire and instruct others to triumph over obstacles.

Most of us are accidental heroes. We pursue a course of action thinking it will lead to fame or fortune or love or the goodies we want, but life rarely unfolds in serenely predictable fashion. It is the nonnegotiable life events—death or divorce, bankruptcy or business loss, a health challenge or a threat to our safety, the long rise to achieve a cherished goal—that require us to look within for the mettle to handle setbacks. Scott Peck's best-selling book *The Road Less Traveled* began with a line that resonated with the collective consciousness: "Life is hard." I recall his saying that the good news is that we improve in our capacity to handle adversity; the bad news is that as we improve, we get more of it to handle.

An essential part of the hero's journey is the return to the community to contribute our hard-won knowledge and wisdom. We return as heroes rather than as victims because we come to understand the tests, trials, and tribulations we endured were necessary to the development of our character and humanity. This growth comes from having altered our perspective of the hurts and disappointments of our lives to transform our wounds into a source of power. Only then can we share the benefit of our experience. In earlier times, indigenous people would sing the hero back to the village. Today, we "unsung heroes," denizens of a far-flung global community that rarely notes our homecomings, have the opportunity to share our stories from the speaking platform. When you become a compelling storyteller of your own hero's journey, you hold the gift of inspiration in your being.

PRINCIPLE #3: *The World We Experience, Both Personal and Planetary, Reflects and Expresses Who We Are Individually and Collectively*

If, as ancient wisdom teaches, the outer world is a reflection of our inner consciousness, then if we want to change the world, we must first change ourselves. Change begins with the recognition that each of us is a complex blend of contrasts—positive and negative, the accepted self and the shadow. Transformation is about recognizing, owning, and integrating these contrasts, not denying their existence or blaming others. Change in the world will come only from many individual awakenings that shift awareness and behavior on a large scale, underscoring the need to give people in your audiences simple actions they can take. Until *we* change, the world we see will remain as it is.

Recently I met with shamanic teacher and author Sandra Ingerman. I asked for her take on the enormous amount of spiritual knowledge being shared today and the sense that many people are waking up to become part of creating a more positive and expansive time for humanity. I wondered, since we are a part of nature with its sunshine and shadows, death and rebirth, and changing of seasons, whether she believes it is possible to transcend the opposites within us. She responded that she had been actively reflecting on the nature of the shadow for seven years. The guidance she has received, she said, is that there is nothing to fear or try to get rid of. "Nature is our greatest teacher," she replied, addressing my earlier reference to the opposites we see in the natural world. She went on to say, "Operating from ego and separation equates to darkness, and while we may aspire to the light of oneness, not many will achieve that in this planet of duality. Our job is to change our own state of consciousness about how we walk in the world and what we put out. The downfall of every teacher is to stop doing our own work."

If you find yourself resisting Sandy's assessment because you think you've reached an elevated state, remember: the human condition applies to you, too! As evidence, watch yourself carefully the next time someone cuts you off in traffic or criticizes or disagrees with you or otherwise incites your ire. Sandy suggests we can't stop the feelings from coming up—we want our negative feelings, after all, because they bring our attention to areas calling for discernment or healing. But just as we can refrain from pushing the "send" button on our computers, we can wisely control and redirect our thoughts, too.

Our judgmental thoughts can be turned inward and cause us to abandon our true work when we allow ourselves to be influenced by what we or others think will "sell." Your clearest and most trustworthy voice comes from your essence, not your ego. Your essence is the real you, which your ego often wants to aggrandize. When you make a practice of going within to ask for what you are to say and to do, you stay connected to a trustworthy source that becomes your ongoing guide to standing in truth and integrity. We must be rigorous in practicing what we preach. Whatever we wish to bring to the world—vision, ideas, or tools—requires that we take the actions we ask others to take. The world will change only as we do.

PRINCIPLE #4: *You Can't Figure It All Out, You Can't Make Anything Happen, and You Can't Make Anyone Do Anything. Every One of Us Holds a Different Strand of the Web of Life and We Each Must Heed Our Own Call*

As we prepare to influence people through speaking, it is easy to think we have an answer for other people—if they would only see it! It is uplifting to find audiences that respond, of course. But often our mission requires that we open up new avenues of understanding and potential support from people whose worldview and values differ markedly from our own. The first step in change is beginning a conversation that introduces a new framework or language. Consider the changes in your own awareness over time and honor what it takes to move to a different point of view.

Knowing you can't make something happen is no deterrent to claiming your magnificence while letting go to the Mystery. Your task is that expressed by cultural anthropologist Angeles Arrien in her book *The Four-Fold Way*, which synthesizes the wisdom of indigenous peoples worldwide in the following principles: First, show up and be fully present. Next, pay attention to what has heart and meaning. Third, tell the truth without blame or judgment. And, finally, remain open to outcome, not attached.

The recognition that we are all connected to something larger as we play our individual parts allows us to hold a deep respect for our tender shared humanity. From that perspective, we can appreciate that mending the web of life is never about what people *should* do. It's about what they're *called* to do.

Transformational speaking inspires others to heed their own call, to do what is theirs to do. It is important to trust that each person's journey will reveal where his or her original medicine can best be applied.

PRINCIPLE #5: *Use Your Authentic Power with Those Who Can Hear You Rather Than the Force of Argument with Those Who Can't*

Authentic power radiates not from position or wealth but from the strength of your being. John Trudell, a poet, writer, musician, actor, and artist and a founder of the American Indian Movement, said in a documentary about his life, "We think power is in government, or military, or education. That's not power. That's authority. Power comes from our relationship to life." His comment resonates with the role of the grandmother council in the Iroquois Nation. The men recommend a law but pass nothing until the grandmothers have met. The question they ask as they assess the value of a proposal is, "Does this support life?" When we affirm life, we stand in authentic power.

The law of attraction suggests we draw to us that which we believe. The state of consciousness we hold carries a vibration that attracts similar experiences. States such as appreciation or anger attract people with a matching "vibe"—whether positivity or "pisstivity." If you come at change with blame and judgment, you'll appeal to other angry people and stir up a firestorm while alienating those who might otherwise get on board. If instead of anger you reach for a different thought, such as the hope held in a better story, you'll approach change in a more inclusive way.

At the same time, there is a place in social change for outrage and the desire to right injustice. I'm thankful for activists who put themselves and their lives on the line to awaken the world to issues that need to be addressed. Once an issue has attention, we can begin the work of understanding, healing, and transcending anger and polarization to build coalitions across society. I notice with my clients that underlying anger are often tears of helplessness and defeat; underneath tears of sadness lie rage and a sense of victimization. Whatever emotion we are feeling deserves expression so we can get to the heart of what is really going on and come to the work of change from a place of self-understanding and wholeness.

In *Power vs. Force*, David Hawkins calibrates the energetic vibration of various worldviews and states of being. He demonstrates that higher vibrations carry more energy, and there is an exponential impact the higher we move up the scale.

This finding underscores the value of applying our energy with people who can hear us and are most likely to act on the call to action we propose. When we attempt to bridge vast worlds of difference, we can end up depleted, feeling like lone voices in the wilderness. The situation is akin to a university professor attempting to instruct a kindergarten class; it is not where she can give the most value. This is not a judgment on where people are—or even a suggestion to avoid groups that are a big stretch for you—but rather an exhortation to apply your energy primarily where you can create results.

Whether or not you accept Hawkins's research as scientific fact, it's a reminder to use the *power* of higher values with people who can hear you rather than the *force* of argument with those who can't. You'll see greater results and find that your successes fuel your impact, making life a lot more fun as you go about the work of change.

PRINCIPLE #6: *You Must Be Personally Sustainable to Do the Work of Change. Cherish Your Precious, Worthy Self*

Extreme self-care and management of your health bring life and vitality to the work of transformation. Visionaries and change agents often ignore their personal well-being, believing there is too much to do and too little time to get the message out. That stance puts us more in our minds than in our bodies, and people can't connect to you through body language if there's no one home. I, for one, am far more inspired by those who radiate joy and hope rather than display the downside of becoming a human sacrifice. Hope is an action plan—not only for those you want to influence but for yourself as well! You must be personally sustainable to sustain the work of change.

As a transformational speaker, what practices might you establish to manage the accumulated stress of your life so you can be fully present and whole in what matters to you? Define and state the truth of what you need to nourish yourself. Mark your commitment to creating vibrant health and a strong spirit by scheduling time on your calendar for that which you know is essential to filling yourself up. Only then can you fully express your gifts.

In addition to your physical body, your energy is a precious resource to be respectfully managed. Many who care deeply take in negativity and stress from others without even realizing what has depleted them. Each interaction with another person or an audience has an energetic component that requires awareness and diligence.

In *Positive Energy*, Judith Orloff, MD, assistant clinical director of psychiatry at UCLA, reveals a type of person she calls an "intuitive empath" and offers a self-test to determine whether this describes you. Consider her questions:

1. Have I been labeled as overly sensitive?
2. If a friend is distraught or in physical pain, do I start feeling it too?
3. Am I drained in crowds, going out of my way to avoid them?
4. Do I get anxious in crowded elevators, airplanes, or subways?
5. Am I hypersensitive to noise, scents, or excessive talking?
6. When I see gruesome newscasts, does my energy plummet?
7. Do I get burned out by groups, requiring lots of time alone to revive?

If you answer yes to any of these questions, it is likely that empathy is compromising your energy. You would think people with these qualities are unlikely to be speakers, but I suspect passion and empathy spring from the same internal makeup. What's more, as we grow in compassion, we become more vulnerable to the kinds of energy imposed by the environments that Orloff describes. Ultimately, deep caring is a compelling call to speak.

Taking charge of our energetic health requires diligence because it is something we are rarely taught early in life. I myself have operated most of my life without recognizing I am a "highly sensitive person," another descriptor of this phenomenon from Elaine Aron's best-selling book series on *The Highly Sensitive Person*. Begin to notice where, when, and with whom you feel chronically depleted and, conversely, where your spirit is enlivened. This awareness, combined with developing personal skills to support your precious, worthy self, will allow you to embrace your mission with joy.

With these six principles as your foundation, you're on your way to becoming a transformational speaker. If you found any of them hard to accept or passed them off as unimportant, note your resistance and see whether you can identify the belief within you that challenges the principle. For example, you may find it hard to acknowledge the idea that the world you experience reflects your inner state, or you may consider yourself too busy to "indulge" in self-care. For now, I invite you to suspend judgment and in the spirit of curiosity apply what I've authenticated. From here, you can begin to claim and trust the person you already are to bring forth the original voice that empowers you to articulate what you— and *only* you—have to say.

2

Be Yourself—
Everyone Else Is Taken

Claiming Your Gifts and Talents

The most memorable communicators step up in their own inimitable way. They avoid formulaic speaking at all costs. They understand that their particular configuration of gifts, talents, and life experiences is unlike that of anyone else. The best they have to give to speaking is contained in their unique perspective. This original medicine, the source of their brilliance, springs from the heart of who they are, creating a singular pattern nowhere else duplicated.

Although most of us have received the advice to "be yourself" at one time or another, the stronger, often unspoken message has been to conform. From the time we're small children, we are molded into being and doing what others expect, requiring us to inhibit the expressive self to fit in. Who hasn't heard the phrases below?

Children should be seen and not heard.

Who do you think you are?

Say please and thank you.

Act nice.

Kiss your aunt.

If you act enthusiastic, you'll be enthusiastic.

Cheer up.

You want people to like you.

Big boys don't cry.

A spoonful of sugar makes the medicine go down.

Don't brag about yourself.

You should know better.

You should be like your . . .

I told you so.

You're too big for your britches.

Whether family, school, or religion, each environment in which we find ourselves has its own conventions that dictate how we should behave. The degree to which these messages are internalized determines how thick the veneer we paint over our genuine expression. Until we are able to stand fully as who we are, these messages, once designed to help us fit in and be accepted (often by those who loved us most), can cause us to approach new situations tentatively, assessing what is expected of us before we step in. Our timidity assures we will not stand out. The other extreme, false bravado, merely masks our insecurities. Either response impairs our capacity on the speaking platform as surely as it does in daily life.

The success of the movie *Little Miss Sunshine,* which won two Oscars, demonstrates our admiration when someone breaks with convention. The film presents a rare example of a child who receives full support for being herself from an otherwise dysfunctional family. The opportunity for a last-minute entry into the finals of the Little Miss Sunshine Beauty Pageant gives seven-year-old Olive only three days to prepare and get to Southern California. Unbeknownst to the viewing audience, Olive's grandfather has been coaching her to perform a sassy stripper routine for her talent. While Olive is backstage getting ready with her mom, the men of the family watch the fierce competition she is about to face. Fearing she will embarrass herself, they rush to her side to lovingly suggest she not take the stage if she doesn't want to. It doesn't even occur to her not to do it and she boldly steps out. As her talent is revealed and she begins to throw her clothes into the audience, the shocked pageant organizers demand that her parents get her off the stage. As her dad approaches, he recognizes that this is a pivotal moment in Olive's life. You can see his dawning realization that he is about to choose between shame and support as he stands behind her while she performs her little heart out. In that split second of decision, he begins to imitate her movements, and soon her mother, brother, and uncle join in the dance, collectively thumbing their nose at expectations as they gyrate off the stage in unison.

Oh, to have that kind of support when an audience is unable to receive us! Yet only you can give it to yourself, and this is easier to do when you are being your real self instead of hiding behind a façade. Gertrude Stein advised, "Beware the double ouch." The first ouch is when we attempt to be someone we're not in order to be accepted. The second ouch is when our true self inevitably comes forward, disturbs our act, and elicits rejection anyway. "Go for the one ouch," Stein wisely urged.

Anatomy of a Bomb

I know of no speaker, myself included, who has not experienced the agony of bombing. My most recent big-time flop changed the direction of my work and my life.

In the spring of 2004 while living in Santa Fe, I was asked to speak to a local group of more than a hundred real estate agents, previously part of two companies, now merged into one. They met weekly in a movie theater. Because of the group's large size and the daunting venue, many agents were holding back from presenting their new listings due to fear of public speaking. My assigned role was to offer a few tips and sign up those interested in small-group on-camera coaching with me.

When I arrived, my contact asked me to sit up in the far reaches of the theater to remove speculation about whether I was a new agent. I complied rather than questioning, one of my first mistakes.

My location hardly primed me to take the stage—in fact, the person welcoming me had to say, "Where's Gail?" I was prepared to work with people who were fearful, but the advance promotion extolling my virtues caused the confident ones to stay on for this part of the meeting, and I suspect they anticipated I would be a feminine version of the boisterous and beloved motivational guru Tony Robbins.

It only got worse from there. I found myself addressing a lukewarm group seemingly uninterested in learning my ideas about how to present listings in a memorable way to other agents. I persevered, telling myself that many audiences love me and simply forget to inform their faces, and I assumed that the people who walked out had previously scheduled appointments. Although I received a polite response, only four people signed up for coaching. That afternoon, the colleague who had referred me removed all doubt about my bombship when he called to say, "I hear it didn't go so well."

The story does brighten, however, because it catalyzed some deep soul searching about where I wanted to show up, how, and for whom. In this particular situation, I had not only accepted a gig with a group about which I knew little, but I was also—at least in my imagination—now the subject of unenviable discussion among people who talk a lot, and Santa Fe is a small town. So I did the practical thing: I hid at home for a week.

While cloistered, I received an email from Tami Simon, founder of Sounds True Audio, announcing the first-ever Gathering of Women Entrepreneurs sponsored by Social Venture Network (SVN) to be held at Hollyhock Retreat Centre on Cortes Island in British Columbia. That invitation was a connection to an audience I wanted to serve. I intuitively knew I was to be there, and if I was to be there, I was to speak. I wrote to Pam Chaloult, at that time the co-executive director of SVN, to propose a program I called "Story Power: Speak Out to Stand Out." Later she said she receives hundreds of proposals and recommendations, but there was something about mine that spoke to her. She knew I was to present.

The next challenge was getting myself to British Columbia. Still reeling from the financial loss of an enterprise my investor partners and I had chosen to dissolve, I nevertheless had to find a way to Cortes Island. I redeemed my last fifty thousand Delta air miles for a ticket to Vancouver, rented a car from there, and camped at Hollyhock to save the cost of a room, freezing my substantial ass.

It was well worth it. There I met kindred spirits in people who stood for change and embraced my approach. They wanted Gail, not Tony. I had come home. Had it not been for my earlier failure, I doubt I would have made the effort to reach out to this arena of change makers where I could be myself in bringing my gifts.

If an audience has a set of expectations—usually unspoken—that you don't match, presenting to them feels as though you are speaking another language without an interpreter. In fact, you are. While you flail valiantly forward, it only gets worse. If this has not happened to you yet, you can be sure it will be part of your initiation. And just as I did, you'll come away from it with both a story to tell and a lifelong lesson about the dreaded double ouch.

Claiming Your Original Medicine

The first principle of transformational speaking as described in chapter 1 is that you are an original, nowhere else duplicated. As I mentioned before, indigenous cultures call these natural attributes and abilities our original medicine. Knowing and accepting your medicine is core to expressing your personal power, strength, and understanding.

To demonstrate the significance of our personal qualities applied to speaking, I ask Real Speaking participants to think of a favorite speaker or a memorable presentation, one that remains with them even years later, and enumerate the qualities that come to mind.

Typically people say words like "authentic," "connected to the audience," "expressive," "expansive," "genuine," "heart-centered," "humorous," "inspired," "passionate," and so on. Rarely do they focus on riveting content or structure, because these are assumed. What's more, studies indicate that the actual content makes up less than 10 percent of a speaker's impact, even though many, unfortunately, stop there. They put something together that's satisfactory, if dull and predictable, and are rewarded with the audience's short applause and even shorter memory of their presentation.

To become a transformational speaker, you need to step from comfort zone to "home zone," from professional to personal, the subject of chapter 4. What will make you stand out are the unmistakable qualities you already possess, perhaps yet to be revealed on the speaking platform. When you can express the qualities of yourself others respond to—indeed, *love* about you—you are stepping into your home zone, the place of your personal power and life experience. You are standing in the power of your original medicine.

On pages 30 and 31 is a list Real Speaking participants have developed in response to the question "What are the qualities of a great speaker?" Rather than simply admiring these characteristics in someone else, consider those *you* already possess. If you embody these attributes off the speaking platform, it is time to share them with your audience.

Once you understand you already possess the qualities you admire to some degree or another, you can more fully step into those you want to cultivate. You can also begin to monitor when you shy away from claiming your power. I learned a lesson about this following a vision quest during which I and thirty others went off on our own to spend four days and nights alone in nature. Upon returning to the group, each person was asked to share his or her experience. During a break after I spoke, one of the program associates commented favorably on my presentation. I demurred.

"Don't you know how magnificent you are?" he asked somewhat incredulously.

"I know I sometimes step into it," I responded. And then with a flash of insight, I added, "Oh, I get it. I step *out* of it."

To assure you don't step back from your own magnificence and to consistently radiate your power, get clear about the definition of your original medicine. At the end of the chapter are some questions and exercises to help you with your definition. For now, choose at least three qualities from the list on pages 30 and 31 that you know are fundamental to who you are and make a conscious choice to fully claim and express them.

Mining the Medicine from Your Professional Endeavors

As you consider the original medicine you are ready to reveal on the speaking platform, take into account the decisions you may have already made to express your professional identity. For example, Houston executive coach and leadership consultant Cathy Nunnally, originally from New Mexico, chose the Zia symbol as her company logo. The image depicts a red sun with four groups of four rays extending from the center and represents perfect friendship between united cultures. In describing its significance, Cathy illuminates an unmistakable aspect of her medicine held in the perspective she brings to her work:

> The symbol of the Zia Pueblo Indians reflects a person's sacred obligations: a strong body, a clear mind, a pure spirit, and a devotion to the welfare of his people.
>
> Four is the sacred number of Zia. To the Zia Indian, the sacred number is embodied in the earth, with its four directions; in the year, with its four seasons; in the day, with the sunrise, noon, evening, and night; in life, with its four divisions—childhood, youth, adulthood, and old age. Everything is bound together in a circle of life and love, without beginning, without end.

Celeste Yacoboni of Santa Fe offers sacred sipping circles to experience the healing properties of plant essences. Her signature workshop, called Becoming the Lotus, incorporates drinking the

Qualities of a Great Speaker

- ❏ Able to laugh at self
- ❏ Alert
- ❏ Alive/liveliness
- ❏ Approachable
- ❏ Articulate
- ❏ At ease
- ❏ Authentic
- ❏ Aware of audience
  - ❏ *Connects with audience*
  - ❏ *Likes the audience*
  - ❏ *Relates to audience*
  - ❏ *Speaks for audience*
  - ❏ *Understands audience*
- ❏ Beautiful language
- ❏ Believable
- ❏ Believes in the message
- ❏ Breathes into the moment
- ❏ Calls forth action
- ❏ Caring
- ❏ Captivating
- ❏ Centered
- ❏ Charismatic
- ❏ Changes us/ increases our awareness
- ❏ Clarity
- ❏ Clear diction
- ❏ Clear-headed
- ❏ Clear message
- ❏ Cohesive

- ❏ Colorful
- ❏ Comfortable/at home with self
- ❏ Compassion
- ❏ Compelling
- ❏ Competent
- ❏ Confident
- ❏ Connected to self
- ❏ Content and structure
  - ❏ *Depth of knowledge*
  - ❏ *Effective presentation materials*
  - ❏ *Familiar examples*
  - ❏ *Good material*
  - ❏ *High content*
  - ❏ *Knows where he or she is going*
  - ❏ *New and exciting perspectives*
  - ❏ *Nuggets of basic wisdom*
  - ❏ *Phenomenal stories*
  - ❏ *Relevant stories*
  - ❏ *Strong ideas*
- ❏ Conviction
- ❏ Courageous
- ❏ Delightful
- ❏ Delivery
- ❏ Desire
- ❏ Dynamic
- ❏ Elegant
- ❏ Emotion-driven
- ❏ Empathic

- ❏ Energized/ energetic
- ❏ Engaged
- ❏ Engaging
- ❏ Entertaining
- ❏ Enthusiastic
- ❏ Entraining
- ❏ Evokes laughter
- ❏ Exciting
- ❏ Expands the mind
- ❏ Expert on subject matter
- ❏ Expressive
- ❏ Exudes eros
- ❏ Eye contact
- ❏ Faith
- ❏ Fearless
- ❏ Feisty
- ❏ Fire in the eyes
- ❏ Flexible
- ❏ Fluid
- ❏ Focused
- ❏ Free
- ❏ Fresh
- ❏ Friendly
- ❏ Generous
- ❏ Genuine
- ❏ Genuine smile
- ❏ Goes with what shows up in the moment
- ❏ Good voice
- ❏ Grounded
- ❏ Has a great time him- or herself

- ❏ Heart-centered
- ❏ Heartfelt/ connection (speaks from the heart, touches the heart)
- ❏ Honest
- ❏ Hopeful
- ❏ Humanness
- ❏ Humorous
- ❏ Impactful
- ❏ Inspires change
- ❏ Inspiring
- ❏ Intelligent
- ❏ Interesting
- ❏ Interesting topic
- ❏ In the flow/moment
- ❏ Intimate
- ❏ Joyful
- ❏ Knowing from his or her core
- ❏ Leaves us wanting more
- ❏ Light and light-full
- ❏ Likeable
- ❏ Likes him- or herself
- ❏ Magnetic
- ❏ Makes sense of chaos
- ❏ Motivates us to change
- ❏ Nonjudgmental
- ❏ Open
- ❏ Organized

- ❏ Original
- ❏ Partners with Spirit
- ❏ Passionate
- ❏ Personable
- ❏ Personal magic
- ❏ Persuasive
- ❏ Playful
- ❏ Poise
- ❏ Polite
- ❏ Prepared
- ❏ Presence: easy to see, hear, and be with
- ❏ Quick mind
- ❏ Reaching
- ❏ Realistic
- ❏ Realness
- ❏ Receptive
- ❏ Relevant
- ❏ Relevant gestures
- ❏ Renewed
- ❏ Respectful
- ❏ Rhythm
- ❏ Risk taking
- ❏ Self-disclosure
- ❏ Sense of drama
- ❏ Sensitive
- ❏ Simplicity of message
- ❏ Sincerity
- ❏ Some movement
- ❏ Spontaneous
- ❏ Sticks to point

- ❏ Stimulates thought and wonder
- ❏ Storyteller
- ❏ Strength
- ❏ Style
- ❏ Suspense
- ❏ Thoughtfulness
- ❏ Thought provoking
- ❏ To the point
- ❏ Touches us
- ❏ Trusts in the moment
- ❏ Truthful
- ❏ Understanding
- ❏ Uses audiovisual equipment well
- ❏ Uses humor well
- ❏ Uses illustrations and examples
- ❏ Varies movement
- ❏ Varies pace
- ❏ Versatile
- ❏ Vibrant
- ❏ Voice connected to rest of body
- ❏ Voice fluctuation
- ❏ Vulnerability
- ❏ Warmth
- ❏ Willing to take a stand
- ❏ Wisdom
- ❏ Words are fresh in the moment

lotus hydrosol and practicing lotus qigong and meditation. When I asked Celeste to explain the significance of the lotus, the way she spoke and moved left no doubt that she holds the medicine of this sacred flower. Here's what she said:

> In the lotus pond I stood, my feet planted deep into the mud oozing with life. The web of roots was so thick my feet became part of this tough woven mesh. My body undulated with the waves of air around me. I reached up toward the sun crowned in the green breathing leaves. There the magnificent pink lotus vibrated with color, life force, sunshine and the buzzing of bees. I disappeared into the stillness of the lotus.
>
> The lotus is an alchemist, its roots in the primal slime, the rich dark earth, and the water absorbing its nutrients. Up shoots the thick stem, its huge green leaves floating on the water. The lotus flower opens to the sun and closes at night, replenishing itself. The buds and seedpods represent the transitions of birth and rebirth, the cycle of life.

Is there a symbol you have chosen to brand your work? Look at it again as an indication of the medicine you bring to your audiences. For example, the Real Speaking logo is a drop of water hitting a still surface that creates an ever-expanding circle. It suggests that the influence of "truth well spoken" ripples out far beyond the words we speak in the moment. Choosing a symbol that aligns with your work speaks volumes about your medicine.

Liberating Your True Self

The ego sometimes rails against a story it thinks is over and wishes to move beyond, particularly one that caused pain or disappointment. This was the case with my friend and colleague Joanne Brem. A top sales executive for a Fortune 500 firm, Joanne had resigned her position determined to find a new professional path that reflected her spiritual development. When she came to Real

Speaking eight years later, she spoke about everything *but* the business career in which she had earned hundreds of thousands of dollars annually in sales commissions. When I asked her how she might apply what she learned from that experience to her new direction as a recently certified professional coach, she studiously avoided the invitation to explore it—that is, until she was delivering the speech she had prepared for the closing session of the program.

Unbeknownst to me, Joanne had brought two changes of clothing in anticipation of her presentation. Along with her flowing feminine garb, which she expected to be wearing, she had packed her trusty business outfit. In fact, she changed twice that morning, first donning what she thought would be her new identity and, at the last moment, changing into her power attire. Claiming her credibility in the corporate arena, she stood to speak about courageously leading change. Just a few minutes into her talk, she hit a wellspring of emotion. As she valiantly attempted to hold it back, I stopped her presentation and asked her what was happening. "What a loss of a phenomenal culture and incredible potential—people like me, all of us! I'm in such grief about what happened to cause me to leave the company I loved!" she exclaimed through her tears and the anger that followed, which demanded release.

That moment of truth liberated her from resisting her true calling. As she opened her heart to her past that day, she took a stand for authentic and courageous leadership, a stand founded on her years of successful business experience. Joanne returned to the world of business to coach executives in building their capacity to lead authentically and retain key employees by creating supportive environments that honor their contributions. The combination of her in-depth business knowledge, her connection to her heart, and her medicine of communication, deep listening, and compassion became the foundation of a satisfying career where she also brings the gifts of her spiritual awareness.

Following are eight exercises to guide you in deconstructing your false fronts to reveal the true self that awaits you and your audience. Remember, it takes understanding and intention to come to a true appreciation of your medicine in a culture that raises both children and sales revenues with the implicit message "You're not enough!"

1. Ask those who know you well to tell you what they see as your innate gifts and talents.

2. Consider these questions: What sets you apart? What is it about you that causes people to listen to you—whether in public speaking or in everyday life?

3. Contemplate this line of poetry from David Whyte: "Anything or anyone that does not bring you alive is too small for you." What brings you alive? Create a collage in answer to that question, clipping from magazines images and words that attract you. Paste them on a poster board and allow yourself to be surprised as they take form. Then speak aloud about what you've discovered.

4. Reflect on this question: When I know I'm not being judged and am unguarded, what parts of myself do I reveal that I really love about myself?

5. Ask yourself: What do I believe without equivocation?

6. Observe those times you hold back from claiming your medicine. What are you afraid will happen? What would likely happen if you didn't hold back?

7. If you've not yet done so, review the attributes of a great speaker earlier in this chapter and consider the qualities you already possess and can therefore bring to your speaking.

8. Write one or two sentences describing what you believe your original medicine to be. Continue to add and refine as you hear words from others that resonate with what you know is true about you and that you want to claim. Then distill this truth—your original medicine—as a simple reminder, such as that voiced by life coach Chuck Roppel, who summed up his medicine as "authentic presence." Janine Stelter-Brolly of Vancouver, holistic life coach and distributor for Isagenix

International, recognizes her medicine as "the wildfire alchemist," reflecting her belief that all life experiences are an alchemical mix to serve transformation.

The qualities that make you a beloved person are also the ones that will make you a transformational speaker. In the same way, your own stories are much more compelling than those you fabricate or learn from others. Linda Solomon, a brilliant writer and mother of two boys, discovered just how compelling her stories are when she began telling her children about her life when she was a kid. She says, "Everything stops when I start telling them my stories. They hang on to every word. They can't get enough of these stories, which I guess is another way of saying they can't get enough of me. Since they are my most important audience at this time, this has been a profound learning for me and helps me to value who I am."

You'll find that adults are no different from children when it comes to loving a good story. If you've not yet courageously looked at the stories of your own life and brought them to your speaking, prepare to embark on an enlivening adventure.

3

God Said, "Ha!"

Finding the Speech You Were Born to Give

The saying "If you want to make God laugh, tell him your plans" kindles a universal chuckle. Who among us has escaped the glaring truth of the statement "Life is what happens when you're making other plans"?

Conventional speech making suggests you can make a plan, find stories that support your key points, and deliver them with aplomb, using all the tricks of the trade. But as in life, so in speaking. The best stories come from your life experience—your fresh, unpredictable, unplanned life experience. Your original stories represent the foundation of your credibility in influencing others. Because they have resulted in the unique combination of life experience and perspective that makes you who you are, they also reveal the most spellbinding speech you can make. Forget finding stories to support your presentations. Instead, work with the stories that have *found you*.

A case in point. Kate Southard, a New Mexico real estate broker and lawyer specializing in water rights, attended my Story Power workshop sponsored by the American Women in Communications in Albuquerque in the spring of 2007. She volunteered to receive coaching in front of the group. A tall, slim redhead, Kate was bursting with creative fire. She also never stopped smiling, even when addressing a serious subject. After I worked with her, others in the group gave her generous feedback about how much more credible she was when her expression matched her words. A woman of action, the next day she signed up for a three-day Real Speaking program beginning that night, wanting to move deeper into what she was learning about herself from that brief coaching experience.

Kate is the funniest woman I know, yet she also has had more than her share of life challenges. During Real Speaking, she explored her more serious stories and learned to align her expression with her words. She left with a plan to get a sponsor for her workshop on women and money, a presentation that reflects her capacity to earn the big bucks and create wealth. Yet her new talk still carried the humor that is her medicine. "Ladies," she advises, "finding a man is *not* a financial plan."

Six months later Kate returned to Real Speaking. She had yet to launch the women and money seminar and suspected there was still some exploration to do about her real message. What's more, she explained, she had come to my class with her best friend of thirty-five years, Cathy, in order to resuscitate their relationship, nearly fatally injured when Kate did not tell Cathy she was ending her twenty-seven-year marriage until after it was over. Kate's trademark happy face had nearly cost her the most enduring friendship of her life.

For two days, Kate did the hard work of digging deep while maintaining her innate capacity to keep us rolling on the floor as joyful recipients of her sidesplitting wit. "God speaks to me through my P&L [profit and loss statement]," she reported, "and there was no money in being the foremost expert on water rights in New Mexico." But she also revealed a more serious side and her internal struggle when she said, "Everyone in this room is doing work that makes such a profound difference. I want to do something that really matters." From Kate's lips to God's ears.

After a guided experience prompting Kate to imagine standing before an audience delivering the speech she was born to give, she appeared disturbed and in deep thought. "I saw myself speaking about water," she reported, "and thousands of people had paid to hear me."

That night Kate left with a heavy heart, preparing to develop her closing presentation that evening. I wondered what would happen. Would she return the next day with a festive presentation or a more somber one that reflected a direction she thought was over and was now asking to be revisited?

She did both. With stories of what she learned about water growing up on a ranch in an arid state, along with deep reflection, hard facts, optimism, and humor, Kate Southard brought alive a timely and necessary subject that on the surface might seem boring and hard to penetrate. And as God laughed with us, Kate was given another gift. One of the "important strangers" in the workshop with her was an individual earning $15,000 a speech for his work with global corporations seeking to minimize their environmental impact. He has become an ally to Kate as she adds to her already strong foundation by researching one of the most pressing issues of our time in order to become a speaker on the international stage.

Our stories reflect the speech we are born to give. In the world of inspirational speaking, the term *signature story* is used to describe the presentation for which a speaker is known, his or her brand in the marketplace. And just as with the fairy tales we loved as children, we want to hear the good ones again and again. The audience may not remember your name, but they will remember your story. You're the Yale-trained MD who learned about healing in Indian Country, the burn survivor in a wheelchair, the POW in solitary confinement who communicated with other prisoners in tap code, the funny Miss America contestant, the *National Geographic* photographer, the woman who wrapped herself in Saran Wrap on a hot Florida day to seduce her husband, only to pass out while he was delayed by a traffic jam. Any veteran observer of prominent inspirational speakers can tell you whose stories these are by these brief descriptions alone.

I once heard a professional speaker actually bemoan the fact that he didn't have a sensational story to help him become rich and famous, as though he would have appreciated having been locked up for seven years in enemy territory or dragged under an automobile for several blocks to boost his career. You don't need a larger-than-life story to reach an audience. The stuff of everyday existence is quite sufficient.

In chapter 4 we'll explore how to tell your stories from the home zone to assure they don't become rote. Your task now is to explore the richest experiences of your life and let the stories emerge that you will be compelled to tell. You'll find they carry the seeds of the message you most want to deliver.

Mining Your Best Material from Your Own Hero's Journey

In *The Path of Least Resistance*, Robert Fritz relates a conversation Gertrude Stein had with a struggling writer who felt he could never write another sentence because, to him, his words felt wooden and meaningless. Stein reminded him that the book he wanted to write

> . . . will come as deep as your feeling is when it is running truest, and the book will never be truer or deeper than your feeling. But you do not yet know anything about your feeling because, though you may think it is all there, all crystallized, you have not let it run. So how can you know what it will be? What will be best in it is what you really do not know now. If you knew it all, it would not be creation but dictation.

The best stories you have to tell are yet to be revealed; otherwise, they would be merely dictation from an old mind-set rather than the wildly creative possibilities available to you as a transformational speaker. You must let your stories run to know what they are. You must dig deep and excavate the life experiences that you may have wanted to bury for all time.

Begin by looking for those moments when you had to be your own hero. Some of your stories will emerge from nonnegotiable life events that arrived like bolts from the blue. Although we like to think that careful planning can insulate us from the vagaries and harshness of life, experience teaches us that the river of challenge flows as strongly as the stream of surprise. Often at the times of greatest hardship, grace steps in and greets us with something that keeps us going—a kindness from a stranger, a new relationship that enriches our lives, an unexpected windfall, a fresh perspective that changes everything.

People need to hear these things. Audience members show up looking absolutely normal—whatever that is—some more so than others. We can't see the greatest act of courage in their day, which may be putting both feet on the floor in the morning and giving it another go. As speakers, we make it a point to look and sound like we have it together, but how much can we learn from those who act as though they arrived in the world with everything figured out, nary a concern or fear along the way? By journeying deep into the well to retrieve the treasure of our authentic self, we discover the parts of ourselves that are truly heroic.

David Whyte, in his poem "The Well of Grief," writes:

> *Those who will not slip beneath*
> *the still surface on the well of grief,*
> *turning down through its black water*
> *to the place we cannot breathe,*
> *will never know the source from which we drink,*
> *the secret water, cold and clear,*
> *nor find in the darkness glimmering,*
> *the small round coins,*
> *thrown by those who wished for something else.*

The best stories are represented by those small round coins that glimmer in the dark places of our lives and wait for us to reclaim them. This is your gold, waiting to be mined.

Stories come from considering not only the turning points of your life but also the people who most influenced you. Who are your heroes? Who are the people who have encouraged you to bring forth your gifts? Who has touched and inspired you along the way?

Let in the New Stories

One of the great things about being a speaker is that you begin to look for the lesson sooner because you know you're adding to your repertoire. You let in the new stories even as you cultivate the riveting standbys. Although you want to be remembered as spellbinding, there's a danger in depending only on well-rehearsed stories to mesmerize your listeners: you may be binding yourself with the very same spell if you allow your stories to become your identity. You don't want to turn into old Gramps still telling the same jokes at the family dinner table, lovingly tolerated but only half listened to. Unless you want to be authentically over the hill or stuck in the past, there's a lot more life in continuing to grow and integrating new material into your presentations. Just be sure to learn the lesson fully before trotting it out for the world!

What's more, make sure the stories you mine from your life experience and tell to audiences reflect a heroic victory rather than a persistent victimization. As cultural anthropologist Angeles Arrien teaches, indigenous cultures observe an agreement that says, "I will listen to your painful story three times. If you come to my door a fourth time with that story, I will turn away." This stance reflects the recognition that listening and compassion are essential—but only up to a point. If we are allowed to tell the same story without ceasing, it becomes part of our identity and may imprison us in an old role, or worse, the mind-set of victimization. Transformational speaking is about the new story, one that asks us to step up and claim our creative potential.

How do we break the spells that convince us our old story is who we are? By trying out the new sense of identity that comes with telling a different story. We are all teachers as well as students in the classroom of life, and trying the voice of an opposite perspective is rich fodder for new material. In communicating, it's not a false identity—it's a different face on the same material. We'll learn more about this when we explore the four disciplines of star quality in part 2.

It Is Not Self-Aggrandizement to Tell Your Story

If you worry that talking about yourself is a mark of self-absorption, relax. Your story is a gift to others, a unique tale that *only* you can tell because you lived it. A story well told becomes universal. It stops being all about you and becomes about the audience and how each person can apply it to his or her own life.

Ann Medlock began the Giraffe Heroes Project in 1984 to foster citizen courage by honoring people who stick their necks out for the common good. After hearing Joseph Campbell talk about the Holy Fool archetype, she realized that the "giraffes" she recognizes are today's "holy fools." The Fool is the most dangerous person on earth, Campbell explained, the most threatening to all hierarchical institutions. He has no concern for naysayers, and no one has power over him. He's not limited, not stoppable, not controllable. He knows what he has to do and he's doing it, no matter what. Ann found that not only did the "giraffe" stories inspire others to stick out their necks where they were called, but also that a story, or even the act of telling it, gives someone a reason to keep going and grapple with a difficult challenge. Never was I more aware of this truth than in 1989 while promoting the book *Beyond Survival: A POW's Inspiring Story* with the author, Jerry Coffee, a retired U.S. Navy captain.

We were in the midst of the Living Heroes Essay Contest, a twelve-city search for middle-school students who would tell us about the heroes in their lives—not the typical rock stars or athletes, but folks close to home who encouraged these young people to bring forth their own gifts.

What began as a book promotion became one of the most poignant experiences of my life. Reading the entries and organizing the twelve events, which sometimes drew hundreds of people to meet Jerry and hear the three winning essays, was deeply moving. Calling the winners and coaching them on the phone was a joy. But most exciting was calling the heroes and reading to them the words the students had written about them. There were usually tears on both ends of the phone line. I remember Lennie, a ballet teacher in New Orleans, as she listened to me read the tribute her former student Stephanie had written. She said, "Thank you for reminding me why I do this. I've been so tired with my other full-time work, I wondered if teaching ballet really mattered." In an instant, she had a better story to tell herself about how much her work meant to her students. It gave her a joyful reason to continue teaching ballet.

Nearly twenty years later, I still remember these kids and their stories. One of them was a young woman who will always be a champion in my mind. I had met two of the three essayists while waiting for the program to begin and wondered where the third was. I was particularly interested in meeting her because she had named *herself* her hero. She wrote that although she had no positive role models in her family or her school, she had maintained good grades and was not pregnant or on drugs. Just as the event was getting started, in she walked with spiked multicolored hair, tattoos, and, as I recall, a piercing (she probably started the trend). She was flanked by two friends who appeared to "have her back." The most noticeable thing about her, though, was *attitude*.

She was obviously stunned she had been selected and looked unsure of how to handle it. As she read her essay, she seemed to dare people to cross her. In the end, she received a standing ovation. Later at the reception, I saw her in animated conversation with several people who were congratulating her. The young woman who left that night was not the same one who came through the door. She later wrote to me and said the experience had changed her life. Until that evening, she had never been acknowledged by adults, she explained. Now she believed in herself as never before.

As she had so bravely asserted, she was in fact a hero. By telling the raw truth and being exactly as she was, she opened the hearts of everyone present and invited in support that was unimaginable to her before that moment. Truly her story will live in my heart forever.

So take the time to find your unadorned truth. "Live the questions raw," exhorted the poet Rainer Maria Rilke. Move beyond your comfort zone to explore the deep questions and wisdom gained from both your triumphs and your defeats. Explore the deep and uncomfortable questions so that someday, as Rilke suggested, you might live your way into the answers. The archetypical experiences of challenge, grief, loss, and victory held inside you can create stories that will resonate in your audiences for years to come. Reveal your own personal truth and those privileged to hear you may forever be transformed.

4

From Comfort Zone to Home Zone™

Expressing the New Edge®
of Emotional Connection

Many speakers think they've arrived when they achieve a comfort zone in their speaking. But that's the exact point where transformational speaking begins to take form. "Comfort zone" denotes ease and relaxation, often at the price of mind-numbing predictability.

The comfort zone is merely the foundation of your speaking. This zone includes the intellectual basis for your presentation. It extends to facts, research, theory, and other sources you may have assembled to make your case or to support your audience in their development. It signals that you are a professional and pre-pared. Mastering the comfort zone meets the expectations of most groups, but if asked later about your talk, they might say, "She did a nice job" or "It was pretty good, I think. I don't really recall what he said." This is hardly transformational speaking.

Beyond the comfort zone, the home zone is the place you go within yourself to find what holds meaning for you in a palpable way that will connect you emotionally to your audience. It may include stories, poetry, music, art, even silence—whatever you choose that bypasses the rational mind and touches people on a soul level. It is the personal, human level of speaking, and it is memorable. It is unexpected because it is rare, but when asked later about your talk, someone from your audience is likely to say, "Unforgettable! Her story brought me to tears, and I'll never see a hungry child in the same way" or "I went to work the next day and asked for a transfer. I was ready to step up to something new that is calling to me." Transformational? You bet.

The home zone signifies an enhanced level of confidence that comes from touching your deepest heart and wisdom and speaking from a place of authentic connection with what lives within you. Being in the home zone tells the audience that you have come home to yourself and are deeply rooted in what you are communicating. From there you create a connection with others where they don't just listen—they *hear* what you're saying. You communicate with people on a soul level so the better story you offer can be heard and acted upon. Just as great literature, drama, and sacred texts bring us back, over and over, to seek wisdom in times of questioning or need, your story can also live on in the hearts of others as an inspiring touchstone. Until you touch people emotionally, a good idea rarely leads to transformation. It remains merely theoretical.

A transformational speech will contain both comfort zone and home zone material. The comfort zone provides the framework; the home zone embeds your message in the consciousness of the audience. Entering the home zone is not an intellectual exercise. You must tell a story that moves you and be willing to reveal your emotions to the audience. This chapter is designed to help you discover the stories that will move you into your home zone. Once you've done this behind-the-scenes work, later chapters will cover how to refine and craft those stories for presentation to an audience.

Accessing Your Home Zone in the Way You Tell a Story

The stories we tell are often a series of facts with little detail to enliven our speaking or touch our own emotions. When we fear our own vulnerability, we avoid the home zone, the place where we can move our audiences with the heroic nature and emotional impact of our quest. Entering the home zone requires that we not just *recall* a story but *relive* it.

The secret to accessing your home zone is not to recite the details of your story from an intellectual distance but to put yourself right back into it and tell it from there. You allow yourself to experience events as they happened. It can be as simple as opening up all your senses as you relive your story.

Vito Zingarelli's mission was to promote the farm-to-table economy on Whidbey Island, Washington, where he makes his home. His pragmatic argument about the need for a healthy, local food supply was interesting but not compelling enough to inspire his classmates in Spirited Speaking, a class I offered at Hollyhock Retreat Centre, to engage in the cause. I suggested he take us into his own garden. Leading us in a full sensory experience, he related the luscious details of each scrumptious vegetable and fruit, lovingly grown by his beautiful wife, Dorit. While we were still drooling, he told us he gets up early before Dorit awakens, takes out the fresh eggs produced by his neighbor's chickens, and prepares a delicious fresh omelet before calling her to breakfast. Now we were really salivating! "It's a good thing Dorit is here with you," I said to Vito, "or every woman in this room would be trying to take you home."

"Why do you think I came?" Dorit said with her sly smile.

When you're exploring access to your home zone, expect challenging emotions to come up as well, and celebrate when they do. Right now this is for you. You may cry, get angry, feel frustrated—in fact, if you really get into this exploration and don't feel anything, you're not working with a story that moves you—and if it doesn't move you, you can bet it won't move your audience. A good story will connect you to your feelings, and there's gold in them thar' hills (and valleys).

Jim, a longtime friend and Southern gentleman beloved by all, attended my hallmark program Real Speaking. When a woman in the group told about being cut off from seeing her nieces and nephews because of her religious brother's judgment of her sexual orientation, I could see that her story incited Jim's ire. When he got up to speak, I asked him to tell the group how Carmen's experience had impacted him. He expressed his anger with strong words informed by his own experience of "men of God" using their spiritual positions to abuse or coerce others, but he wasn't able to let the force of his feelings support his voice. He knew he was suppressing a strong emotion that begged to be released, yet he also feared his own rage. "You don't want me to go there," he said.

"There's a safe way to do this," I told him, but he wasn't convinced. When I respected his request to back off, he looked me in the eyes and said softly, "Help me." With that appeal, he allowed his deep feelings to rise up in his body and find expression, first locating the place in his gut where they resided, then giving them a sound, then letting them out. The physicality of the release of years of repressed fury was stunning. In fact, a body worker to whom I had referred him saw him both before and after the program and later said to me, "Whatever happened over those four days, a different man walked through my door. People are so frequently retraumatized by old memories, but he released what he was holding on to." What a privilege to support Jim in the work that freed him to connect with a longtime but forgotten passion that enlivened his life.

In the early stages of Real Speaking, people usually haven't planned what they'll talk about. This is by design to allow new material to take form as the person naturally discovers what wants to be said—the material that scripting and rehearsing often silence before it has a fighting chance to be heard. When Linda Solomon got up and found herself talking about being in New York City on September 11, she began to weep. Other feelings followed, including shame at commanding the full attention of the group, then the unexpected sensation of standing in her truth and power as she experienced how captivating it was to the audience when she spoke from a place of deep emotional honesty.

When you allow yourself to relive the story, it is not a dramatic recitation. It is not a set of facts put together in a pleasing way. It is not just a snippet of information to illustrate a point. It is a riveting, soul-inspiring, from-your-heart, sometimes in-your-face, vulnerable form of expression. It takes you to a New Edge of expression that moves you from comfort zone to home zone. Don't shut yourself down by saying to yourself, "What does this have to do with my speech?" Suspend judgment and let it fly. When you find yourself hitting a bulwark of emotions, feel where it resides in your body. Give it a sound, even if it can't be put to words yet. Or put your hands over your heart, breathe in to it, and ask for the courage to express what's beneath those strong feelings. Remember, this is not yet meant for prime time, but you'll be much closer to finding your most moving stories.

There Is a Place for Strong Emotion and Tears

Clients often tell me they avoid relating emotional stories when speaking because they're afraid they'll cry or even scream. Rather than backing off from raw expression, recognize that your stories must take you down a path of feeling or they've likely lost their impact. When working with material that evokes strong emotions, begin alone or with a few supportive people. Withhold judgment about where and how you will apply what comes up. If you decide to use what you discover, your strong feelings will only fuel its impact. When that is no longer the case, it's time to find new material.

For example, my home zone story of my growing friendship with my dad after my mom's passing, his hilarious and heartbreaking reentry into the world of dating, and his sudden death in an automobile accident always brings tears to my eyes. When I look around the room, men and women alike are crying and laughing with me. Why should we be ashamed of our feelings about something as universal as the loss of our parents? Your capacity to move an audience is directly linked to your willingness to express the emotional impact of your experiences.

Another example of this truth came up at a Real Speaking program when I asked participants to name the impossible thing they want to accomplish by five o'clock. Al said his was to speak about things he cares deeply about without "welling up."

"How about accepting that you'll well up and that it's a powerful part of your expression?" I responded. Others in the group enthusiastically concurred, stating that when Al revealed his vulnerability they found him especially compelling as well as more present and accessible.

"You got me!" he chuckled and allowed himself to go even deeper into his exploration. By the next day, he was telling his story using the complete range of his emotions, from the despair of a scandal that had humbled him and brought him to his knees, to the full expression of his love for his family, his community, and his world. As he spoke, his medicine of magnetism and compassion that gives permission to others to celebrate life and contribute by embracing what they love was palpable.

Al's willingness to convey both his playfulness and his abject sorrow and regret illustrates how enlivening it is for others when we express the fullness of authentic expression. Falling Awake founder Dave Ellis suggests that many people maintain a narrow emotional bandwidth that prevents them from feeling either ecstatic joy or profound sadness. Ellis calls people with a severely limited range of emotional expression "flatliners." In speaking, that translates to a monotone, boring presentation.

Becoming a Witness to Your Own Hero's Journey

The five stages of the hero's journey, as described by Joseph Campbell, can support you in expressing the emotional truth of your experience. They also provide an effective framework as you move toward organizing the structure of your story in a talk. Each stage suggests questions to ask yourself as you mine the gold in your own stories so you can later decide whether you want to share them with an audience.

1. *The "call."* There is a separation from the ordinary as you set off on your quest, a departure from life as you have known it. What led to this situation? Was there a sudden change in your life? Did you *want* to leave the ordinary behind, or was the call forced upon you?

2. *The journey into the unknown.* What shifted to make this an unexpected journey instead of a normal event? What about it was unknown, unfamiliar? Who were the key characters? Recall them in rich detail. Have at it by using their voices, facial expressions, and body language so you can later embody the people you mention in your talks.

3. *The challenge.* What obstacle did you encounter? How did you feel—shocked, vulnerable, confused, frustrated? Allow yourself to express your response as you felt it in the moment.

4. *"Slaying the dragon."* Against all odds, you overcame the obstacle. How did you persevere? What negative aspects of yourself did you have to face and integrate? What support from unexpected sources did you receive? How did you turn your pain, trauma, or challenge into a source of power? Experience your process, your insights, the conquering of self-doubt and confusion, the excitement of discovery.

5. *The homecoming and sharing the discovery.* What is the memorable aspect of the journey? What is the wisdom gained, and how has it changed your life and the way you view it? How will you share it? What do you hope others will gain from it?

To identify what you've learned from your own hero's journey, relive it first and express it aloud. From there, you might videotape it. Each version will draw out more material as you allow yourself to fully experience your story instead of simply recalling it. Let your body move with the telling. As you do, you'll find it holds the memory of details that will surprise you. Remaining engaged with your body is also the secret to keeping a story alive on the speaking platform. As you allow new aspects of the story to come to you in the moment, you'll tell it in a fresh and genuine way each time.

Remember, sharing the discovery is a significant part of the journey. Your experience must be witnessed by others for you to complete the hero's journey and provide the service to which you have been called.

Revealing the Hidden Framework of Perception

Once a client who enjoys analyzing structure took me to lunch following a program I'd just given. "OK," said Pat, "I watched you all weekend and I don't know how you do what you do because you worked with each person in a different way. You must have a formula. What is it?!" There is no linear formula, I assured her, only active, compassionate listening, a deep desire to be of service to people who want to grow, and an intuitive sense of which door to knock on to help people open to themselves.

Nevertheless, I yearned to be able to explain what happens in Real Speaking that moves people into their magnificence. Then, in 2006, I attended a daylong workshop with Dr. Alberto Villoldo, a psychologist and medical anthropologist who has studied the spiritual practices of the Amazon and the Andes for more than twenty-five years. Author of *The Four Insights*, he presented a framework for healing that corresponds to the way I teach speaking. His stunning capacity to make visible the invisible structure that supports healing can be applied not only to enhancing the medical model but also to catalyzing positive change through speaking.

Mainstream medicine addresses physical symptoms with prescription drugs and/or surgery, Villoldo pointed out. These interventions are designed to mask symptoms or fix something that needs physical repair. But what happens, he asked, when we attempt to address symptoms through the mind, as happens in successful psychotherapy? By beginning to think in new ways—mind over matter, as they say—it is possible to influence our physical health.

The level beyond the physical and mental is the domain of the soul, familiar to the shaman. The soul is moved to a response by story and song, art and poetry, ritual and ceremony. When feelings and emotions are touched, the mind and the physical body are also influenced.

Beyond the level of soul, the shaman intervenes at the energetic level, the place of spirit. Villoldo explained that shamans call this the "luminous energy field," and an intervention here can cascade down through the soul and mind and heal the physical body.

The higher the level at which the shaman intervenes, the greater the opportunity for healing—or in the case of speaking, the greater the potential for transformative change. It is a person's soul that will hear and be moved to act on something that resonates as truth. The mind will only hear the words and evaluate, then become absorbed in something else. If you think your mind is your greatest faculty, take into account who is telling you that. And the body—well, it likes its familiar patterns and habits. If a good idea changed that, we'd all be off processed sugar and eating organic produce, in season, from local farmers.

A compelling example of using story and song to touch the soul is the prize-winning video that documents Bob Bossin's original song "Sulphur Passage" used in the twenty-year initiative to save Clayoquot Wilderness in British Columbia from logging. Bob believes in the importance of the arts in telling the story but didn't know until years later that the first thing the campaigners did in its crucial meetings to influence the customers of Canada's biggest forest company was show them *Sulphur Passage*. "It was perfect," recalls Tzeporah Berman, one of the leaders of the market campaign. "In four minutes, it showed them what clear-cut logging looked like; it showed them that we weren't just a few environmental zealots—there were thousands of us. And it was moving. I recall the vice president for purchasing at a big Japanese company watching with tears in her eyes." View the video at www.bossin.com and you'll understand why. That video opened hearts as well as the door to victory.

From Information to Illumination

Applying Villoldo's levels of perception to public speaking, the literal level is that of **information**. It informs the *Activist*, who perceives a symptom, a dis/ease in society that needs to change. The message? Wake up and change what you're doing.

The level of the mind is that of **insight**. It informs the *Advocate*, who asks, What information can I provide to change your mind so you will grasp the importance and think differently about this issue? Sparking insight stimulates a desire for change.

The level of the soul is that of the **imagination**, or the *Artist*. Here we experience the power of story, song, poetry, art, and ceremony, forms that bypass the rational mind and touch us emotionally. Being touched at the soul level moves us to act because we hear a call to align with something greater than ourselves. "Imagination is everything," Einstein told us. "It is the preview of life's coming attractions." This is where the information and insight we've gained are most likely to be implemented.

The level of spirit is one of **illumination** and is the place of *Awareness,* which is beyond words. As we transcend the limits of our bodies, minds, and emotions, we are transported into the presence of the sacred. Those rare moments fill us with new energy and remind us of what is possible. Speaking to the power of the nameless, Rumi touches on the fullness of the world of the spirit where there is no separation from others in the following poem, as translated by Coleman Barks:

> *Out beyond ideas*
> *of wrongdoing and rightdoing,*
> *there is a field.*

I'll meet you there.

When the soul lies down
in that grass,
the world is too full to talk about.

Ideas, language
—even the phrase "each other"—
do not make any sense.

In those moments of illumination, we understand that what we most want is already available. The experience of our essential selves allows us to revel in a story of oneness that has become our reality, however fleeting. It inspires us to do whatever it takes to enter that kingdom again.

From Story to Storyteller

Alberto Villoldo's one-day program became an invitation to change my life. He explained that at the level of the physical, we have a story. It is typically a story of victimization in which we get stuck if we fail to see our predicament or pain as a call to the hero's journey. Our willingness to transform our wound into a source of power is what moves us from being a hapless victim of circumstance to becoming the storyteller of the hero's journey.

My participation in the workshop with Alberto inspired me to embark on a course of training, Healing the Luminous Body, with the Four Winds Society. The promise of the first week was that I would shed my old story the way the serpent sheds her skin: all at once. This appealed, because I was tired of the one-painful-scale-at-a-time approach. I wanted the freshness and vitality that had eluded me as I worked hard to make the inner changes I hoped would transform my outer reality. My health had me down and financial stress had exhausted both my bank account and my adrenal glands, resulting in a persistent sense of fatigue. At the time, I had an "ain't it awful" story going that many of my friends were retiring just as I was starting over. The only thing that was going to make the substantial tuition of the program worthwhile was ridding myself of my old story in one fell swoop. It was a tall order, but I was prepared to fully engage and allow a miracle to happen for myself. And it did.

As speakers, we run the risk of relying on "yesterday's masterpiece," a phrase for which I credit Alexander Shaia, author of *Quadratos: Beyond the Biography of Jesus,* who realized that it was time to give up a story that had sustained him for years and progress to the level of expression that called him now. Persistent reliance on an old story keeps us from moving forward. Embarking on the journey of embracing a new story can push us into the life we were born for and start us on an adventure rich with the challenges we need to evolve.

Dreaming the New Story

Where do we find the new story inside ourselves that will give us hope? Dreams and daydreams, with their bounty of images, offer hints of where to begin. A new story came to me through a dream.

In my daytime musings, I was concerned about some health issues and what my future years might hold. A recent bone density test had signaled problems. In my dreamtime, I found myself on a bustling city street looking for a traffic signal where I could safely cross. Approaching an intersection, I noticed a very old woman with a cane, bent low with osteoporosis, waiting for the light to change. I rushed to her side to provide support in crossing. As I moved toward her, I found myself looking into blue eyes that literally danced with life, set in the most vibrant face I'd ever seen. Then, she took *me* by the arm and guided *me* across the street.

This new story transcends the decrepitude of aging. What if we trusted that within each of us there is an ancient knowing waiting to direct our steps into new and unexplored territory? It asks only that we take it by the hand and let it move us into the unknown parts of ourselves that are ready to be expressed.

Elevating the Possibilities

When we pose questions to an audience, the answers we get depend on the level of perception from which we speak. Buckminster Fuller said, "You never change things by fighting the existing reality. To change something, build a new model that makes the existing model obsolete." That is a call to tell a better story than the ones told before.

What story keeps you going? What vision do you hold that is so powerful and palpable it burns off your exhaustion and puts a song in your heart? What story brings you alive with joy at the thought of it?

If we are to inspire change, we must reach for a story full of promise. Rumi said, "Move from within. Don't move the way fear wants you to . . ." Tyrants and demagogues attempt to scare people into action—or away from it, as the case may be. Don't dwell on how bad things are unless you want to keep them that way. Many of us know how challenging our current times are. Despite the difficulties, we need to believe that what we do can make a difference, even if it is a small one. We also need to believe that, against all odds, we might very well make a big difference. We need to be reminded of our power as individuals. This is the beginning of transforming the critical mess to a critical mass of change makers who can use storytelling and myth to shift public policy as well as consciousness toward the betterment of all human beings and life on earth. It is up to each of us to tell the best stories we are capable of.

Recently a story found me. I was half-listening to a speaker, deciding whether I wanted to commit a weekend to his workshop, when he drew me in with a brief tale about a warrior who loved the earth and whose tears brought rain. When I asked the speaker to repeat the story, he said it had come to him in the moment, then vanished. So I continued the tale myself. It goes like this:

> A warrior who loved the land was brokenhearted about the drought that withered the forests and the valley he called home. He worried, he prayed, he walked around looking at the devastation, stewing about it as the earth became parched and his people starved. Finally in desperation he threw his arms around the trees he loved and began to weep. As the tears spilled from his eyes, the dry ground responded. It plumped up and kissed his feet. And the heavens, who loved him too, rewarded each tear with an hour of life-giving rain.

Recently I tried something new by asking a class to develop a new story together. I began with, "There was a warrior who loved the earth" and invited them to add to the tale. As each person thoughtfully added his or her piece, a beautiful, collective story to which we were all connected evolved. Later, in a class of twelve people who shared a fear of speaking, I began with, "Once there were twelve brave people who banded together to make a difference in the world, even though they were terrified about speaking out." The healing story that emerged, as each person added to it, elevated us all to a new level of courage and connection with each other as allies in the work of change.

Stories are everywhere. Begin with your own, then see what else comes to your door. You may find that all you need is an opening sentence to ignite a blaze of creative possibilities.

Your Core Message

Now that you have reflected on the heroic nature of your own journey and allowed the emotional impact of your stories to inform you, remain in your home zone and ask yourself this question: What message has emerged that comes from the heart of my being?

Until you have answered that question, you are not ready to speak, not until you are absolutely clear about your core message. Your core message is the one thing you must communicate no matter the audience, no matter what you are asked to speak about. For many people, getting to this is challenging. "I have so much to say," my clients tell me. Likely you do, too. But your core message is central to your original medicine, and once you find it, it will become the organizing principle for everything you say, and everything you say will have a distinct purpose.

Ask yourself, "If I had only one minute to speak, what would I say?"

If people get really stuck with the one-minute message, I say, "This is it. You're in your coffin about to be buried. You sit up and say what it was all about, the gift you were here to express, and the difference you wanted to make. Go!"

For example, my core message, in its simplest expression, is "Be yourself—everyone else is taken." If I have a full minute to expand it, I let people know they have a magnificence to be expressed through speaking that will bring them and their audiences alive and fuel change in the world. I suggest they rarely know their best material because they have shut it off, wondering whether it is appropriate rather than embracing it because it is real. I emphasize that speaking becomes fun and enlivening for an audience only when we allow that same spirit to flow through us; further, it offers the possibility for transforming what people believe is possible because we signal a better story, one that inspires people to step forward in a new way to be part of a growing cadre of change agents. That community support is necessary to fuel our capacity to remain strong. When you're dying, you don't want to wish you had stepped out of your self-imposed coffin and given it all you've got. Be inappropriate, if that's what it takes, but say what you came to say.

My clients and I are always amazed at the clarity that emerges in this casket communiqué. Some experts suggest you write your own eulogy and see how you want to be remembered, but I've found the pressure of speaking our last words even from an imaginary coffin provokes the recognition that we don't have forever to grapple with our core message. After all, it is central to who we are and why we want to speak.

The intention of this chapter has been to move you into the full awareness of how your life experience has shaped you and the message you are called to share. Take the time to define both your essential message and the story from which it took root. Express it to someone close to you and allow it to touch your souls. Then you'll be ready to move from core to craft as you expand your capacity to present *your* truth, well spoken.

Part 2

THE **ART** OF
TRANSFORMATIONAL
SPEAKING

**Connecting with
Your Audience
to Catalyze Change**

5

Truth Well Spoken

Mastering the Four Disciplines
of Star Quality

Finally—you get to stop the inner exploration and practice the speaking skills that count!

The disciplines outlined in this chapter require that you become aware of your speaking habits so you can integrate the changes you wish to make as a natural part of your expression. Begin applying these skills *now* to enliven your communications every day, even before you develop and deliver a presentation. Include them as you explore your stories and bring them into your daily conversation. If the rigor implied by the word *discipline* turns you off, consider its root meaning: a "disciple" unto oneself. That's the inner call to excellence that will support you in becoming the catalyst of the changes you most want to effect.

Most speaking coaching programs begin with identifying and practicing skills, asking you to present your material so you can improve it. It is my ardent hope that you recognize by now that starting with skills development is likely to move you further away from your magnificence rather than closer to it as you impose one technique after another over an already less-than-confident persona. Yes, you may already be a very good speaker, but if you're reading this book you're looking for improvement at some level and likely don't know your best material. If you *are* an accomplished professional, your challenge is likely about overcoming "jet lag" in your life journey to let the person you've become catch up with you and find its voice.

The home zone, presented in chapter 4, is the foundation from which your speaking will advance in a single bound. When you express what you have to say from a place of genuine connection with yourself and your story, most of the skills you need are already in place. That's why I so frequently hear people tell me they're great when speaking one-to-one and in small groups but that they lose their capacity in front of a large audience. When you're "home" with friends and colleagues, your volume varies according to what you are speaking about, your gestures are natural when you leave your hands free to move, your eye contact is authentic, and your body language matches what you are saying. That's because you are coming from what's real rather than an idea of what a speaker is *supposed* to do. Your assignment now is to bring that same ease to the speaking platform by making a few small adjustments in your everyday communications.

At a class where I suggested our skills will serve us whether we're speaking for two minutes or two hours, Emily Medvec of Prudential Real Estate had an "aha!" moment, reporting, "I just realized *anytime* I'm talking, I'm speaking." Remember Emily's insight, and recognize that each communication, beginning now, is an opportunity to apply these disciplines and expand your capacity to be heard. Think of each person to whom you speak as an "audience" of one and have fun with this. Yes, you heard me right: *fun!* Consciously "playing" with these skills opens up your communication in ways that are exciting and expansive, if you allow yourself to be exuberant and even stretch what you think are your limits by not holding back. It has worked for me and my clients. In fact, in my three-day Real Speaking trainings, we begin applying these skills to all our communications long before we move into presentation development.

The First Discipline: Vary Your Tempo

The tempo, or pace, of your speaking allows people to track your words and take them in. Whether you talk rapidly or slowly, the key is to vary speed. A shift in pacing can wake people up, just as a sudden silence can cause an audience to sit on the edges of their seats to hear what you will say next. (More on this in tool #2 below.)

TOOL #1: *The Much-Maligned Period*

End your sentences. This is not as easy as it sounds. Listen to yourself and you will discover just how difficult it can be. I've coached people who can talk about a wonderful subject for five minutes without inserting a period. By the end, the audience is lost. Completing every sentence is a simple tool that will instantly improve all of your communications.

Often I resort to reminding clients of the grade-school lessons I grew up with. Thankfully, elementary education today goes beyond the white middle-class world represented by Dick, Jane, Sally, and Spot, but those of us who grew up with these texts still remember them, largely because of the short, choppy sentences: "This is Dick. This is his sister Jane. Their little sister is Sally. They have a dog. The dog is Spot. See Spot run." When you use short, concise sentences, you force yourself to pause, and this allows your audience to absorb your words. It will seem difficult and contrived at first, but it really works.

One Real Speaking participant found a creative way to address this speech pattern. On the day of his presentation, he wore a polka-dot shirt to remind him to insert periods!

TOOL #2: *The Pause That Refreshes*

We've all heard the pause for effect, contrived for the purpose of manipulating an audience's emotional response. Yet this orator's tool can be used as an authentic expression from your home zone. When you are "home," you will naturally pause to reflect or to allow the enormity of something to be absorbed by both yourself and your audience. Again, the key is variety so people stay with you. A pause signals what you most want others to consider. It is also a stunning substitute for filler words such as "and" and "so" and sounds such as "uh" and "ummm." It is much better for an audience to perceive you as thoughtful rather than out of touch or lost.

TOOL #3: *Slow Down: Home Zone Ahead*

You've heard speakers who naturally speak at a very fast clip. John DeMartini, the prolific author featured in the best-selling book and video *The Secret* comes to mind. He knows this about himself, so he uses it as an opportunity for humor by asking, "Am I speaking fast enough, because I have a lot to tell you!" Vancouver sustainability strategist Coro Strandberg talks very quickly and can be so funny that you hang on for the ride because you don't want to miss a thing.

Many of us tend to talk too fast when we feel nervous, with the goal to get through this awful thing as fast as possible. Wrong! Slowing down allows the depth of feeling you have for your subject to surface. It is especially vital when you are in your home zone.

I found DeMartini a bit suspect when I first heard him because he looked so coiffed and well dressed in an off-white suit that I couldn't imagine he was real. His constant use of sexual innuendo completed the picture of a not-altogether-trustworthy dude. After a break, someone asked him to tell his story. To my surprise, DeMartini went directly to his home zone. He told of the learning disability that caused him to drop out of high school and of the fateful moment when, homeless and hopeless, he met his mentor at a free lecture at a yoga center. In time, his mentor convinced him that he could prevail in the education system. The story of his journey of successive failures and eventual successes, authoring more than a dozen books, evoked great emotion for us because it did for him.

He slowed down in the telling of it and allowed his tears to flow, removing all doubt that his high energy and commitment to his message are real. He later apologized for the sexual references, suggesting that those who talk about it likely aren't doing it, which relegates his comments to the category of "oral sex."

It is crucial to slow down when you want to make a point that is central to your message. If you're a fast talker and find yourself moving quickly through a central theme, slow down right then and there and r-e-p-e-a-t it e-v-e-r so s-l-o-w-l-y. Otherwise, it will get lost in your runaway speech pattern to which people entrain and zone out. Until you master your pacing, your speaking will lack the punch it needs to bring your core message home.

TOOL #4: *Resume Speed*

If you're a slow talker, the practice of picking up your tempo is also very important. The suggestions to come in the third discipline, verbal punctuation, will help you find a different voice, essential to keeping your audience with you. If you loll along at a snail's pace, the audience will begin daydreaming, engaging with their own mental chatter, which is much faster than the speed of the sound of your voice.

The Second Discipline:
Align Tone of Voice with Your Message

The tone of your voice communicates more than the actual words you speak, and if they are contradictory, tone trumps intention. Your audience will hardly trust your concern about the future of the planet if you talk about it in an upbeat fashion with a huge smile plastered across your face. Nor will they believe you if you tell them you are enthusiastic using a morose tone of voice that suggests you're about to go down to the morgue and tell them you're ready.

TOOL #1: *Use a Higher Voice Tone When . . .*

. . . you are expressing excitement or enthusiasm or sharing good news. A high voice tone is appropriate to the following messages:

- A wonderful thing happened today! We got the grant!
- I'm so happy to hear that your speech knocked them alive!
- The United States finally signed on to the Kyoto Treaty. Hooray!

TOOL #2: *Lower Your Voice Tone When . . .*

. . . you are expressing concern or alarm or announcing sobering news. A low voice tone is appropriate to these messages:

- I don't know where the funding will come from to keep this project going.
- The polar ice caps are melting.
- Our leader has been arrested for posting pornography on our website.

TOOL #3: *Avoid the Valley Girl Syndrome*

This one is my pet peeve. The speaker makes a statement, then strips it of its power by ending it with a question mark: "I went into town to confront him?" "This is what I know needs to happen?" Inherent in Valley Girl–speak is an apology. The tone undermines the message.

Dawn McGee, a financial genius who was helping an entrepreneur establish financial projections for a new venture, thought all was in place for a dynamic presentation to the bank. Dawn accompanied her client and reports that everything went beautifully until the banker asked, "How much money do you need to do this?"

"Oh, about $50,000?" Dawn's client responded, putting a question mark on her financial requirements. She did not get the loan.

Standing in front of a group of people, women must remember that they are fully empowered beings capable of introducing powerful ideas and commanding attention. Women must remember that they are not seeking approval and take a stand in the full power of their conviction. This stance is communicated through your voice tone as well as your posture and presence.

The Third Discipline:
Add Verbal Punctuation

Just as a written sentence requires punctuation so the reader can follow the writer's meaning, the spoken word also requires that you punctuate with your voice.

TOOL #1: *Emphasize*

Lift a word out of a sentence. Let it stand out from the rest of the words around it. This signals that you assign importance to that particular idea or phrase.

For example, read the following sentences aloud, emphasizing the capitalized word or words:

It SIGNALS to your audience to what you assign greatest importance.

It signals to YOUR AUDIENCE to what you assign greatest importance.

It signals to your audience to WHAT you assign greatest importance.

It signals to your audience to what YOU assign greatest importance.

It signals to your audience to what you assign GREATEST importance.

It signals to your audience to what you assign greatest IMPORTANCE.

Emphasis is an essential tool when you use a statistic. If the stat is important enough to include in your speech, it bears emphasizing with your voice and sometimes with restatement. For example, "Eighty-two percent of managers in Canada are looking for other jobs," reports Alanna Fero, who leads a Vancouver consulting and search firm. "That's four out of five top staff members."

TOOL #2: *Use Verbal Commas and Exclamation Marks to Accurately Communicate Your Meaning*

Consider this headline: "Child, dead at 91." Although I read the obituary because I was curious about what I thought was a misprint, the newspaper was actually reporting on the death of Julia Child. Here's another example from a professor who asked a class to punctuate the following sentence. "Woman without her man is nothing." The men wrote: "Woman, without her man, is nothing." The women, on the other hand, stated, "Woman! Without her, man is nothing." Adding commas and exclamation points communicates your meaning while livening up your language so you won't sound monotonous.

TOOL #3: *Speak in a Voice That Matches the "Face" You Want to Put Forth in Your Content*

Expanding on the second discipline—aligning your tone of voice with your message—consider the part of you from which your content arises and speak from that voice and its corresponding face. It doesn't work to smile when you're telling a story that broke your heart. Don't frown when you talk about the wonder of the sky at dawn.

Angeles Arrien notes a tribal teaching that asserts that you remain alive to your life only when you express three "faces" in your communication: the faces of the child, the young lad or young maiden, and the elder. The integrated adult expresses all three.

The face of the child conveys wonder and curiosity. Jennifer Chapman of Wild Planet, a toy company, understands the power of this expression. At each staff meeting, she reads a letter from a child to remind them of their real customers and the reason they are in business.

The child's face on your communications would likely be paired with a slower tempo, for example, as you express awe in describing a breathtaking landscape or moving moment. Dr. Brian Nattrass, a sustainability advisor to many large firms such as Nike and Starbucks, expresses the child's face of wonder when he speaks of the birth of his daughter, an event that shifted his life direction from corporate lawyer to planetary change agent. "From the moment I witnessed Sarah's birth and held her to my heart," he explained, "I knew I had to do what I could to assure she grows up in a beautiful and sustainable world." Then, moving into the face of the young lad seized by creative fire, he continued, "I passionately wanted to become an effective agent for change in icon organizations— believing that if they changed, they would help shift the culture." His career course correction moved him to the face of the elder, where he expresses his love and his wisdom.

The child's face is often the hardest for adults to access. For a primer in recapturing what it has to teach you, rent Walt Disney's *The Kid*. The film stars Bruce Willis as an uptight image consultant approaching his fortieth birthday when he is visited by himself at age eight. If you need a nudge to remember your kid and your lost dreams, this movie will take you there.

The face of the young lad or maiden reflects a person burning with zeal. This voice often causes you to pick up your tempo because it is bursting with creativity, eros, and inspiration, giving life to ideas and dreams. Both Coro Strandberg and John DeMartini, mentioned earlier in this chapter, reflect this face with ease.

The voice of the elder reflects deep wisdom, born of life experience. This face is usually thoughtful and deeply grounded in knowing what it knows, having seen what it has seen.

The elder is also called the face of "rude magnificence," a phrase I love. In 2005, I presented a keynote address and a workshop in Geneva, Switzerland, for the Women's International Network, a stimulating business gathering that annually attracts hundreds of women from forty-five countries. After the conference, my friend Runa and I took a trip around Lake Geneva, then checked into the inexpensive accommodations I had booked only to discover we were in a youth hostel. After a leisurely dinner nearby, we returned and found the lobby, which adjoined our room, full of young people listening to loud music. We went to our room to assess the situation, quickly proclaiming it "deafening." Because Runa had two teenage boys, I suggested she would be more skilled than I in getting the kids to quiet down. I followed her back to the lobby as moral support and noted the music was coming from a radio behind the desk on our side of the room. As Runa prepared her opening remarks, I walked to the radio and, without saying a word, shut it off. We returned to our room and collapsed onto our beds in uproarious laughter as we imagined them saying, "Now that was an act of rude magnificence!"

It's important that you *be* the face you are expressing rather than use words that convey these characteristics, just as when you share your story you *be in it* rather than *talk about it*. These faces of curiosity, passion, and wisdom are typically natural among friends. The stretch can be mustering the courage to reveal our many dimensions when standing before our audiences. A client I went to hear speak a year after his Real Speaking training had become such an excellent speaker, I asked him, "How did you integrate these skills so masterfully?"

"By using them every night when I read bedtime stories to my five-year-old son," he responded. "While working with the skills you taught me, especially verbal punctuation, I found a lot of humor rising up and it made me comfortable sharing that part of myself in my speaking."

The Fourth Discipline: Enliven the Voices of Your Inner Selves and Characters

This discipline will put you on the fast track to improving your speaking, on and off the platform. It will move you from somber to scintillating, morose to magnificent, boring to bitchin'. It's about putting expression into your speech.

There is only one tool for the fourth discipline: *When you intro-duce a character, move into his or her voice and body language.*

You yourself have a preferred voice that is a result of what you have learned works for you in the world. It's not even necessarily the real you, but it got you this far, so you're unduly attached to it. Perhaps you found acceptance by expressing invincibility and strength, so you learned that voice well. If you discovered you could get through tough situations by pleasing and appeasing others, you perfected those voices. Perhaps diffusing a difficult situation with humor has been your specialty.

The problem is, whatever the pattern that gains us the acceptance of others, we run the risk of letting it become who we think we are. "The Mask worn after the face has grown becomes a wall that rubs and cuts," Rumi writes, speaking to the pain of remaining in an identity we have outgrown. If we are not willing to move to another expression, we become boringly consistent in the way we approach our lives and the people in them. Over time, we silence the voices that can bring us fully alive, on or off the speaking platform.

Your speaking will progress dramatically when you are willing to reveal the real voices that live inside of you. Why be an automaton when you can enjoy the amazing diversity that is you and you alone? Sure, you may have your confident and commanding voices that help you maintain control, but ceaseless self-assurance keeps people at a distance, too. Maybe you long for the courage to move beyond crowd-pleaser and conformist because there's little real intimacy in your life. Perhaps you're tired of being the life of the party and would like to turn down the volume in order to invite people to come closer.

We each embody many voices, those of family members, teachers, lovers, partners, and all the other characters, imagined and real, whom we have known and loved or struggled with since coming into this world. There are many other voices that are uniquely yours to express. They represent your singular life experience and your original medicine. They comprise the package that is

uniquely you. You have within you voices of longing and belong-
ing. Passion and compassion. Reverence and irreverence. Love and
loss. Outrage and frivolity. Belief and grief. Vulnerability and victimization. You also embody the guiding voices of intuition and
spirit. As these and other voices are invited forth from within you,
you'll find they have much to say to inform and enliven your life
and your speaking.

The poet David Whyte, in his exquisite poem "Sweet Darkness,"
writes, "Anything or anyone that does not bring you alive is too
small for you." Voices bring you alive!

Here are three simple ways you can experiment with voices
to get started on this surprising adventure of discovery and self-
expression.

1. Review the list on pages 75 and 76 of dozens of voices that Real
Speakers have identified, confirming the infinite possibilities of
moving into the expression and body language of the people who
populate your stories. Decide on a sentence you'd like to experiment with and speak it in a variety of voices from this list or your
own list. Have fun. To get started, how would you sing "Happy
Birthday" in the voice of a villain? A biker chick? An evangelist? A
cowboy?

2. Assume the voice of the person you are talking about when you
tell a story. When you want to show your audience how rude the
clerk really was, demonstrate the attitude you witnessed. When
you share a tender moment, move into a softer, more loving voice.
Don't tell us about a song without at least humming a few bars—
or belting out the whole tune. You don't have to be a singer, only
willing to risk showing the audience your vulnerability, thereby
giving them permission to experiment. I once took a drumming
workshop from a sophisticated, very together woman. Only when
she began to sing, in a most unfortunate cadence, did I have the
courage to step in with my own not-ready-for-prime-time voice.

Show us a bit of each character and your own character as you
introduce them. Just as you reviewed the qualities of great speakers

Voices

Abuser
Academic
Activist
Addict
Adventurer
Advocate
Aggressor
Alchemist
Angel
Antagonist
Appeaser
Artist
Athlete
Authority figure
Bad boy
Biker chick
Bimbo
Bleeding heart
Born-again
Bottom-liner
Broker
Buddhist
Buddy
Buffoon
Businessman
Caregiver
Caretaker
Catalyst
Champion
Change agent
Charmer
Charming
   bastard
Chauvinist
Cheerleader
Chicken Little

Child
Chosen one
Class clown
Coach
Columbo
   (pretend you
   don't know)
Comedian
Comic
Commander
Conductor
Controller
Counselor
Country boy
Court jester
Cowboy
Creator
Critic
Crone
Crusader
Crybaby
Damsel in
   distress
Dancer
Dealer
Destroyer
Dictator
Director
Diva
Don Juan
Dragon slayer
Drama queen/
   king
Dreamer
Drill sergeant
Driver

Drone
Earth mother
Educator
Entertainer
Entrepreneur
Evangelist
Exhorter
Expert
Facilitator
Fanatic
Father
Feminist
Finder
Fire starter
Flag-waving
   patriot
Follower
Fool
Friend/pal
Fundamentalist
General
Glamour girl
Goddess
God's voice
Good daughter
Good girl
Good mother
Good old boy
Goody-two-
   shoes
Guru
Gypsy
Hard worker
Healer
Helper
Helpless female

Hero
High priestess
Holy boy
Humorist
Hussy
Iconoclast
Idealist
Idiot
Ingenue
Inner child
Inspirer
Intimidator
Jock
Joe Cool
Journalist
Judge
King
Know-it-all
Lady's man
Leader
Lecturer
Liar
Liberated
   woman
Life-of-the-
   party
Linguist
Live wire
Lone wolf
Lord of the
   universe
Lost child
Lotharió
Love child
Lover
Macho dude

(continued)

Voices *(continued)*

Magician
Man's man
Marketer
Martyr
Mechanic
Mediator
Medicine man/
  woman
Minister
Model
Mom
Monk
Monkey wrench
Motivator
Ms. Cool
Mystic
Narcissist
Negotiator
Nerd
New-Age seeker
News com-
  mentator
Nice guy
Nun
Observer
Optimist
Orphan
Outlaw
Overachiever
Parent
Party girl
Patriot
Patronizer
Peacekeeper
Peacock
Perpetrator

Persecutor
Pessimist
Peter Pan
Philanderer
Philanthropist
Philosopher
Pied Piper
Pimp
Playgirl
Playmate
Policeman
Politician
Pontificator
Preacher
Predator
President
Priest
Priestess
Prince
Princess
Professional
Professor
Promoter
Proselytizer
Prostitute
Protector
Psychic
Queen
Questioner
Rabble-rouser
Racketeer
Ranter
Realtor
Rebel
Redneck

Rescuer
Rising star
Risk taker
Rocket
Ruler
Sage
Salesman
Savior
Scared wolf
Scholar
Seductress
Seeker
Senior
  statesman
Sensitive man
Servant/server
Shakti-energizer
Shopaholic
Smart-ass
Snag (sensitive
  New-Age guy)
Snake oil
  salesman
Son
Sophisticate
Sorceress
Southern belle
Spinner
Spiritual
  director
Sports fan
Sports hero
Sprite
Star
Starlet
Stud

Sugar daddy
Supportive
  spouse
Survivor
Teacher
Tease
Teenager
Temptress
Therapist
Tough guy
Tree hugger
Trickster
Tyrant
Underachiever
Vamp
Victim
Villain
Visionary
Voice in the
  wilderness
Warrior
Whiner
White knight
Wife of . . .
  (lovely/
  beautiful)
Wild child
Windbag
Wise elder
Wise guy
Wise woman
Witness
Wizard
Workaholic
Wounded child
Zealot

in chapter 2 to see which ones you already possess, see how many of the voices listed lurk within you, waiting to be expressed.

3. Identify the voice with which you usually communicate. For example, are you typically the leader, the visionary, the expert, the teacher, or the comic? In what ways does this persona support you, and in what ways might it be limiting you?

As you consider these four disciplines, you'll likely find that one or two are easy for you and are already a natural part of your expression. Choose the one that requires the most attention and track your use of it. You could even tell a friend or colleague what you are working on and ask him or her to remind you. I've found that one small change—for most people, the capacity to end a sentence before starting a new one—will literally transform your communications. Keep in mind that your most important practice is to stay "home" and connected with what you want to convey.

Once you enliven your voices, they'll have so much to say you'll never lack for material and an enticing way of presenting it. Then your task will be to distill it. In the next chapter, we will explore what you need to know about your audience so you can do just that.

6

Know Thyself,
Then Thy Audience

Preparing to Be Surprised

You've worked to develop great content, and you've explored what's yours to say. How do you condense all your wisdom
and knowledge and stories into one transformational talk?

You don't. Now it's time to heed the words of Buddha: "Better
than a thousand words is one word that brings peace."

David Whyte says it another way in his poem "Loaves and
Fishes":

> *This is not*
> *the age of information.*
> *This is not*
> *the age of information.*
> *Forget the news,*
> *and the radio, and the blurred screen.*
> *This is the time of loaves*
> *and fishes.*
> *People are hungry,*
> *and one good word is bread*
> *for a thousand.*

One word, you ask? But I'm making a whole speech!

Your One Good Word
Is Your Core Message

Now that you've done the work to excavate your original medicine, your core message, and the characters that populate your life, you're in a position to decide what your one good word is. The "word" takes us back to the importance of your core message, the one thing you must communicate no matter whom the audience, no matter what you are asked to speak about. Perhaps by now you've found the signature story from which your core message evolved. The rest is supporting material.

In part 1, you were asked to bring forth your core message as your "casket communiqué." Forget for a moment that burial in a coffin is not an earth-friendly way to dispose of your remains. Breathe into your heart and consider at this moment in your life what you would say to the world if you had only one minute to speak. Rilke said, "Go into yourself. Find out the reason that commands you to [speak]; see whether it has spread its roots into the very depths of your heart; confess to yourself whether you would have to die if you were forbidden to [speak]."

When Harmony West, creator of the *Bless You, Mom* card deck, stood up to speak at a Spirited Speaking class, she got to the part of her message where she wanted to express her strongest beliefs about motherhood. Then she suddenly stopped mid-sentence. "What is happening right now?" I asked.

"I don't know. What I wanted to say went away. I felt like something just went through me," she responded, making a gesture that suggested a spear going through her belly.

I told her my clients sometimes report memories, whether from ancestral lineage or previous lifetimes, of persecution, facing a firing squad, being hung, burned at the stake, or otherwise put to death for their beliefs. As Harmony considered this possibility, she summoned her power and, taking command of what had stopped her, moved forward with her message with confidence. As often happens, our exchange inspired someone else in the class to jump up after Harmony had finished and move to the front of the room and announce, "I'm next."

"I get what's going on with the constriction in my throat," he said, "and I'm going to stop being tentative and making light of my message." My brief discourse with Harmony spoke volumes to Charlie about a subconscious memory that was holding him back, and he broke through to claim new ground for his future direction.

Even today, with our assumed freedom of speech, many people have qualms about expressing their beliefs due to the political climate. Others are very public and suppress nothing, both online and face to face. Whatever your core message, it requires that you take a firm stand.

Here's Where We Switch— It's Not All About You

Now that you've identified your original medicine and core message, it's time to consider your audience. What are their reasons for coming to hear you? What is their probable receptivity to your message?

The best-case scenario is that they are hungry to hear you, that your talk will be bread for a thousand. May you have those occasions where the heavens open and angels descend and your audience gives you the kind of response that will fuel a thousand more speeches.

Whether you're a big name in speaking or relatively unknown, the audience will be made up of people who are asking themselves, "What's in it for me?" It's analogous to the Gary Larson cartoon with the caption "What does your dog hear when you speak?"

And then the answer: "Blah, blah, GINGER. Blah, blah, blah, blah, blah, blah, blah, blah, GINGER."

It's the same thing with any audience. Unless something you say has their name on it, it's all blah, blah, blah to them. Just because someone is sitting in a seat doesn't mean he or she is tuned in to you. It's your job to make sure people are listening by making your words both personal and universally meaningful.

One participant in my Speaking Out for Change class insisted that his audience couldn't hear what he had to say. He felt discouraged about making an impact even though he was passionate about his message. I invited him for coaching in front of the group. "First," I suggested, "consider those of us in this room to be the audience you want to address and tell us why we can't hear you."

"You are classically trained economists. I'm an environmental economist," he said looking around the room. He paused for about three seconds and then said, "Already you're thinking I'm not a *real* economist."

Bingo! He grabbed the attention of everyone in the room. In that moment, he met his audience where they were, which was wondering what this defector from the mainstream could possibly teach them. He demonstrated a perfect opening in just a few words. Consider your listeners and address up front any objections they may have to what you have to say. For another group, an audience of people concerned about their environmental impact, for example, his opening would be very different. This is one reason why canned speeches just don't work.

Coaching this man was so much fun. He had already been introduced to the concept of voices, and when I asked him to talk about the point at which he departed from traditional economics training, he recalled an incident with a professor who espoused a theory that caused another student, a dear friend, to leave her study of economics for good. With a little encouragement, he *became* the professor, allowing us to eavesdrop on the classroom in an entirely captivating way. The voice was funny and recognizable as the monotonous lecturer, but the story itself brought him to the edge of tears, along with the rest of us in the room. He was definitely in his home zone.

When he came to expressing what he wanted from us, that we make decisions about economic growth based on the impact on the planet and not just the financial bottom line, I asked him to tell us about areas of his own life that were destructive to the earth. He shared his struggle on the micro level in an authentic and heartfelt way as he told about a cheap fare that allowed him to travel overseas, a flight he could never have afforded had it been priced to capture the real cost to the planet.

This ten-minute coaching session demonstrated several of the key components of a transformational speech:

1. Be absolutely clear about and committed to your core message.

2. Meet your audience where they are.

3. Include yourself in the challenge you are addressing.

4. Know how your message benefits your audience and why they should care about what you have to say.

5. Identify what you want your audience to experience so you can create the mood of your presentation accordingly. For example, do you want them to have fun and get involved? Slow down and get into a reflective state? Experience their creative gifts? Leave energized with a specific commitment to put into practice?

6. Know what common ground you share with your audience and where you likely already relate to each other. Building on this creates connection.

7. Anticipate the unquestioned beliefs and assumptions you may be challenging. These "psychological contracts," often unconscious until they are activated, must be addressed or everything you say may be discounted. For example, I once went to hear a highly recommended speaker who, early in her talk, said we didn't need to be concerned about taking care of the earth because it would take care of itself. After that statement, I was assessing my own response and unable to follow her into the territory for which she is known for making a contribution. She lost me with her opening comments. Don't make the same mistake by tossing off glib

remarks that show you are out of touch with the people you want to reach.

8. Relay the good news, particularly if your talk has to do with naming the bad news. What is the way out? What is the better story?

9. Know the story from your life that fueled your core message, and determine which of your many other wonderful stories are relevant to the points you want to make.

10. Identify what you want people to do differently as a result of your presentation and let them know how to take action.

In order to best plan for these ten components, find out as much as you can about who will be attending your program by consulting with the person or people who have engaged you. They should be able to define what is expected of you. If they aren't able to articulate this, it behooves you to ask good questions. Here are some important questions to get answered:

- What is the nature of the gathering?
- How many people will be attending?
- Who will be in the audience and what are their challenges?
- What are their expectations?
- How much time do I have to speak?
- What happens before and after I speak?
- If it is a panel, who is the moderator? How is it organized?
- What result would the organizers like to see from my talk?
- How will we know whether or not the talk was a success?

If you don't already know what the group is all about, visit the website and review their publications and other materials. Ask the organizer for names of people who represent a cross-section of the audience. Make appointments to speak with them by phone. Although hearing what the leaders have to say is helpful, talking to other folks who will be in the audience will give you a sense of what to expect and likely garner some good stories as well. What's more, making these personal connections will give you the added benefit of meeting people in advance by phone who consequently will be primed to listen.

Silent Dynamics and Values Differences

The people in charge of the event often don't know what the audience wants. They know what they themselves want to see happen, but that is not always what the people in the audience will respond to.

Whatever the audience you are addressing, don't make the mistake of prejudging them as a certain "type" of people who likely won't share your values or perspective.

One of my clients, Marc Rosenthal, is a prominent Austin, Texas, trial attorney. Marc's medicine is that of a gentle warrior. After working with me, delighted to learn to speak from his heart without sacrificing intellectual content, he began recommending Real Speaking to other members of his firm. His law partner, Lynn Watson, didn't want to come. Marc finally ferreted out the reason. She thought the course would be a dull review of tired technical "rules" for public speaking. When she ultimately reluctantly decided to come, she was elated with her experience and acknowledged Marc, who is a bodybuilder, as a man whose "biggest muscle is his heart." Lynn herself gave one of the most memorable speeches ever at Real Speaking in the form of a closing argument of a trial that left no doubt of her heart and humanity.

Gerry Spence, a celebrity member of the legal profession, wrote *How to Argue and Win Every Time,* a book I bought years ago when I felt I was the underdog in a critical negotiation. Imagining I would learn how to be uncompromising, I discovered instead sage advice from a principled man who promotes truth telling and mutual gain.

Spence has become one of my personal heroes. His turning point story in *The Making of a Country Lawyer,* his autobiography, is worth much more than the price of the book. Early in his career, representing insurance companies, his job was to keep financial judgments to a minimum. One fateful day he defeated an old man who had worked all his life and was hit by a drunk driver. Thanks to Spence's courtroom skills, the old man was denied his claim. All those years of waiting for the payback of a happy retirement came to an end when, after months of hospitalization, the final medical report said he would never get any better. It was over for him, except for the pain.

But it was the last case Spence ever argued for an insurance company because he was forced to confront the consequences of what he had done. After the trial, he went to the grocery store to fill his grocery cart with the fixings for a victory celebration. Standing right in from of him in the check-out line was the old man he had defeated. When the man turned around, painfully, Spence saw in his pale blue, watery eyes his own beloved grandfather. It was a haunting moment. As he stared into those eyes, he asked himself, "Is it my job to cheat old men out of justice?" The experience changed his life and led him to become the champion of the oppressed in cases that would eventually make him famous, such as the Karen Silkwood case.

Spence came to view his insurance clients as having "ink for eyes and digits for souls"—the same reason many distrust the corporate world. Fortunately, today many companies embrace the triple bottom line of people, profit, and planet. When they don't, keep in mind that audiences consist of individuals who may actually be misfits in a particular corporate culture. Ipsos, the global market research firm, surveyed senior managers in Canada and found that 82 percent are seeking new jobs. Lack of alignment with organizational values is likely at play.

Your job as the speaker is to inspire change, and change begins with individuals who need to know where to start. Give your audiences something to say yes to. Your mission may be to change an economic system that undermines values you hold dear, and unexpected as it may seem, you're likely to discover global change agents in the highest echelons of corporate life.

The designation "cultural creatives" (CCs) originated as the result of a ten-year demographic study completed in 1997 by Paul Ray and Sherry Anderson of Stanford University. Whereas demographic studies are usually based on specific identifiers such as gender, age, race, income, and geography, Ray and Anderson discovered a large, unrecognized group equally represented across all classifications (except for gender; at the time of the study, 40 percent of cultural creatives were male, 60 percent female). The researchers chose the name to indicate people who were changing the culture. They described CCs as individuals who share a common worldview, values, and lifestyle that embraces whole systems—the ecological, economic, social, and spiritual dimensions of how things should function in a healthy and sustainable culture. Because the popular media infrequently recognize these issues, CCs often think they are alone, the scholars found. *The Cultural Creatives: How 50 Million People Are Changing the World*, published in 2000, reminds us that cultural creatives "would likely be a more potent force if they could see how promising their creativity is, or know how large their numbers are. These optimistic, altruistic millions might be willing to speak more openly and act more confidently in shaping a new way of life."

When your desire for change impels you to action, there is comfort in knowing there are legions who share your values. You just may have to be the first one to speak out.

Different Thinking Styles

When something needs to get done in a fast-paced environment, the go-getters typically name a problem and decide on a course of action to solve it. This approach does not always lead to the best or most inventive decisions because people who need to explore emotions, meaning, and purpose before they get on board are left out of the decision-making process.

The Institute of Cultural Affairs, as part of its excellent training in group facilitation in which I participated, teaches a discussion method called ORID, a structure for effective communication that broadens perspectives and offers the potential for meaningful dialogue. ORID stands for objective, reflective, interpretive, and decisional or, as those of us studying it called it, *what?*, *gut, so what?*, and *now what?* Although it was designed for those leading conversations, ORID represents a winning formula for speakers who want to stimulate inquiry in the minds of audience members.

At the objective, or *what?*, level are the facts. Attention is on the basics, such as what people see and hear. This is where you provide the intellectual foundation of your speech.

The reflective, or *gut*, level stimulates emotional responses. It allows space to feel anger, excitement, and fear because people are reminded of a past association. Telling stories invites the audience to enter the reflective level.

At the interpretive, or *so what?*, level are values, meaning, and purpose. It brings up for people the significance they attach to a subject, even the story out of which they live. Asking questions such as "What does this mean to you?" and "What might this mean to your business?" stimulates personal interpretation and inquiry.

The decisional, or *now what?*, level, so common to our goal-oriented culture, is where individuals decide their relationship and response to the topic. It suggests next steps and asks people to take action.

A transformational speaker knows that inclusivity is paramount to getting people on board. By consciously incorporating material that appeals to all thinking styles into your presentation, you will speak to the entire audience, not a chosen few.

Other Differences within Audiences

In addition to diverse perceptions, values, and thinking styles, every audience represents varying learning styles as well as cultural and generational differences. Lisa Berg, president of One Global Bridge, recognizes that differences have deep layers. Her international work, especially with indigenous peoples, has resulted in an understanding that everyone has a different experience of his or her own inner life that informs and shapes his or her worldview. Working with leaders, she offers the wisdom of many perspectives, emphasizing the importance of a depth of knowledge of oneself and an expanded appreciation of multiple ways of knowing. If you use nonlinear ways of accessing information, such as visualization, looking for signs in nature, dreamwork, or paying attention to synchronistic events, you may strike a resonant chord with others who appreciate a multidimensional approach. If you suspect such an exploration would be a stretch for your audience, be sure to offer stories and data about the validity and effectiveness of these methods in providing highly creative solutions to longstanding challenges.

Truly, there are enough unknowns in any group to make the most courageous speaker quake—unless, of course, you recognize that transformational speaking is not about changing who you are to fit in. Understanding differences so you can discover how to best bring forth your original medicine while meeting the audience where they are is the goal. With each speaking experience, you will move closer to learning where you can contribute the greatest value while experiencing the greatest joy.

Now that you have enhanced your understanding of the ten components of a transformational speech and the differing values and learning styles in any audience, let's move on to crafting a masterful presentation.

7

Look, Ma—No Script!

Crafting a Masterful Presentation

Using the guidelines of transformational speaking, never again will you have to painstakingly write out a speech, nor will an audience have to endure the result as you read it to them word for word. Never again will you need to memorize any text but the occasional quotation or line of poetry you wish to include. In fact, if you were in my class I'd *forbid* you to write your speech. I absolutely discourage it, and here's why.

You know your material. You have great stories. You now understand the home zone. You know you have to show up and be present. You know your audience and how to connect through tempo, tone of voice, verbal punctuation, and voices. Does it begin to make sense that a written script is exactly what you *don't* need? You need a structure, yes, but you must allow for spontaneity within it so you can connect with your audience in the moment and respond accordingly.

Organizing for Spontaneity

You can't script spontaneity any more than you can fake sincerity. Knowing the key thought or story you want to express allows you to enter your home zone and speak from your heart. You may use a familiar story, but the telling of it will be fresh because you move into the experience and relive it. Trust that your audience will appreciate and trust off-the-vine produce over canned corn.

The small but mighty sticky-note allows you to carefully craft your structure while liberating you from ever having to write out another speech. The process begins by identifying a large blank space to become your "storyboard." It could be a door, a wall, a window, or a flip-chart page. Choose something you will pass by frequently as your presentation takes form. Next, write your core message, in its simplest form, on a sticky-note and place it at the top. Then jot down each key idea you want to include, one per note. A thin-tipped black marker works well because the line is bold enough to see at a distance. If you're an experienced speaker, you will already have core content for use as possible modules; make a note for any that complement this presentation.

One of the beauties of this system is that you have a place to put each new thought and idea as the speech takes form. The ideas you post may be random at first, but the system assures you will capture what you most want to include. If you start your storyboard a week or more ahead of the presentation, you'll be quite familiar with your content by the time you take the stage.

Once you have several sticky-notes placed on your storyboard, start moving them around to group associated thoughts. You'll find that once you begin to work on the organization of your talk, it begins to work on you. You'll find yourself reflecting through the day. Hmmm . . . maybe this would flow better if I put it here instead of there . . . how's that transition from one principle to another? . . . is that the best story I could tell for this audience? . . . does this material I've used before really fit, or is it yesterday's masterpiece? . . . do I emphasize my core message more than once, in different ways?

Throughout the process, ask yourself, "How can I provide *insight*, not just *information*? How can I really *connect* with my audience?"

Elements of a Great Presentation

Great presentations take many forms, but several key components deserve advance preparation. As you work with your storyboard, consider the following guidelines to discover the format that best expresses your original medicine and core message.

Opening from Your Home Zone

The purpose of the opening is to grab the attention of the audience. It is designed to intrigue them, wake them up, and answer the question "Is this worth my time?" Choose something that will put you in your home zone, because once you're there, it's much easier to maintain it than to find it later. You can begin with:

- a story
- a provocative question
- a startling statistic
- a quote from a respected member of the group
- a song, chant, or prayer

Don't begin with a joke. Someone will likely have heard it and label you as out of date and lacking creativity. (More on that later in this chapter when we look at the use of humor, which should be original and natural.) And never begin a talk with "That's a tough act to follow." It is always a privilege to follow a wonderful speaker because that sets a positive field for you to step right in to. Saying "that's a tough act to follow" undermines your own original medicine just as you're stepping up to the platform. (The only time I heard this statement work was at the 1980 Tennessee Women's Career Convention. Barbara Gardner Proctor, a dynamic African American with a message to match, preceded a business speaker named Casey Wondergem. When Casey took the stage, he shook his head in an expression of awe, and said, "It's hard for a brother to follow a sister like Barbara." His self-effacing humor and genuine appreciation of Barbara opened the audience to what he had to say.)

Elizabeth Clearwater, a life coach and psychotherapist of Chippewa-Cree descent, leads ceremonial song circles. She begins her talks with a quiet moment followed by a chant that comes from deep within her being. As the sound resonates throughout the room, she sets the space for something profound to happen. The energetic shift is always tangible and the audience's rapt attention is instantly assured.

Dr. Robyn Benson, asked to speak at the 2007 Bioneers conference about personal sustainability and health, began her talk with a simple question and waited for the answer. "How many of you in this room are living at optimum health?" she asked.

My alter ego Madame Ovary takes the stage in sexy Victorian lace and with a saucy attitude quotes Uruguayan journalist Eduardo Galeano, who, at a Lannan Foundation Lecture in 2006, proclaimed:

> Medicine says the body is a machine.
> Marketing says the body is a business.
> Religion says the body is a sin.
> The body says, *I am a Fiesta!*

Be creative with your opening to make it evident that you are original and something significant is about to happen. Your job is to challenge your audience to think something they haven't thought before or feel something they haven't felt before, as Dave Ellis, Falling Awake Coaching founder, describes his objective with audiences. Avoid starting with something your audience is likely to have heard before. Go to new territory that will capture their attention. If you need to cover dry or familiar background information, do it later or provide it in a handout. And make sure you answer the question they are already asking: "What's in this for me?"

Your Signature Story

Your core message emerges from a life experience that created the stimulus for what you want to say. It is what confers you with authority. You've enriched your story with enlivening details; now it is time to deliver it in a way that inspires your audience, allowing them to identify with you and remember the heroic nature of their own journeys. Make sure the lessons you share exemplify exactly what you want to teach. What is the point of the story and how does it apply to your audience?

When your audience connects with you emotionally, they are most open to receiving what you have to say and making a change or a decision. So, in addition to your information and perspective, your stories are what allow the audience to move into their imaginations and make the experience their own.

Key Points That Include Spellbinding Stories and Compelling Information

Typically you will cover two to four points, using both spellbinding stories from your home zone and compelling information from your comfort zone. For example, if your book offers twelve dynamic principles to conquer complacency, a one-hour speech might include only four of these principles, devoting fifteen minutes to each to describe and reinforce it in multiple ways with stories, examples, application, and participation. (Here is where you use the stories and examples of other people who have inspired you; if it's all about you, it becomes a turnoff to your audience.) Avoid information overload. The audience can't assimilate it. Instead, refer people to your book or provide a handout covering the remaining principles.

Signature Statement to Emphasize Your Core Message

To reinforce your key points and make them memorable, find a phrase that concisely communicates your core message. Mine is contained in the sentence "Be yourself—everyone else is taken." If I open with this, repeat it a few times during my talk to reinforce later points, and go the further step of closing with it, my audience will remember my core message even if they forget everything else

I've said. Don't force this; let it emerge as your audience members tell you what inspires them. When it's right, it will be unforgettable. Dr. Martin Luther King Jr.'s poetic words "I have a dream," President John F. Kennedy's statement "Ask not what your country can do for you but what you can do for your country," and Barack Obama's "Yes we can," immortalized them as visionary leaders. Once we become clear about what we wish to be known for, each of us has the ability to speak eloquently and poetically, delivering our signature statement in a way not easily forgotten.

The Better Story That Inspires Reaching for a New Possibility

A transformational speaker always leaves an audience with a better story, something it can reach for in creating a new experience. What story do you suggest and how will you weave it? What is the future we can cocreate as we reach for this new possibility?

Audience Involvement to Draw on the Wisdom of the Room

There is always great wisdom in the room, and speakers who know how to draw it forth can create magic. By encouraging a response from the audience, it is possible to add to the momentum of the talk and deepen its meaning. When people can explore ideas that are forming and speak out, they are less likely to lose the inspiration of the moment.

Just as important as getting people talking is setting parameters that will help them know when to stop. Time is limited, so if you ask people to speak, make sure you are ready to manage the time and let them know when you need to move on.

A simple way to stimulate creative conversation is to ask people to pair up. Then pose a provocative question for them to discuss. Ask each pair to decide who will respond first. Explain that you will signal the beginning of the conversation with a bell, chime, or even

Reassurance!

a whistle, depending on whether you like to enchant or referee. Tell them when they hear the sound, the second person should begin speaking. To make sure everyone has equal time, come prepared with a timer, a watch with a second hand, or a stopwatch.

Afterward, ask for volunteers to speak about their experience. In a large gathering, prepare for this in advance by setting up microphones in the aisles or assign someone to pass a mike. Be specific about the response you want: Did anyone find him- or herself on the edge of a discovery? Did anyone come up with a new idea on how to address the issue at hand?

Then move the conversation into new territory. Ask questions such as "What stops you from enacting solutions?" "Where are you stymied?" or "What is your next step?"

Ask for clear statements with no more than one minute of background and explain that you will ring the bell when the minute is up. Preparing people by stating the rules ahead of time takes the charge out of applying them.

In-the-Moment Coaching to Demonstrate Principles

Coaching of a volunteer is another way to demonstrate the application of the principles you recommend. Early in your presentation, you might say you will ask for a volunteer later so the delayed processors in the group can decide whether they would like to come forward; otherwise, they may not have time to respond. Although they rarely speak up right away, because they are considering several perspectives and possibilities at once, delayed processors may well be the most creative or thoughtful people in the audience. When you extend a nonthreatening invitation to participate, several people will probably volunteer. Select intuitively. Just follow your gut and your choice will probably be spot on. Twice, coaching as part of a presentation did not work well for me, and both times I'd selected a "volunteer" in advance. I have learned to trust that the dynamics of the moment will nudge the right person to the front of the room.

Just as with audience participation, set ground rules when coaching an audience member. This is particularly important if you suspect a participant may "over share" about something very personal. For example, when I teach the home zone, I've discovered that people will sometimes take a great deal of limited class time to share material that is emotionally raw. These stories are not appropriate to use as a coaching opportunity for public speaking. Now in my short classes where time is at a premium, I ask for a story that volunteers want to use in their speaking for which they have emotion but not unfinished business.

Call to Action to Invite Change

Typically, you want your audience to do or see something differently as a result of your speaking. It may be to laugh at themselves, change their behavior, extend themselves to write a check to support your cause, or contact you to learn more about your product or service. Perhaps you want to introduce them to the beauty of an idea and inspire an epiphany. Perhaps you want them to buy your book. When there is something specific you want them to do, be sure to ask.

In the mid-1970s, one of the first motivational speakers I heard was Zig Ziglar, the dynamic sales trainer who made an art form out of motivational speaking. I recall buying an expensive set of tapes on sales techniques after he enumerated what a person will spend to prepare for a sales call—the price of the suit, the haircut, the car wash, the briefcase, and more, totaling hundreds of dollars. His call to action was "After all that investment, isn't it worth $50 to have these tapes to know what you're going to say when you get there?"

At the conclusion of *An Inconvenient Truth*, Nobel Peace Prize–winner and former Vice President Al Gore provides a myriad of simple steps anyone can take to make a difference. He tells us there is still time if—and *only* if—enough of us decide to act.

Inspirational Closing to Fill with Hope

Your closing is where you reinforce the story of a new possibility both to challenge your audience and to fill them with hope. Your goal is to leave them on a high note, ready to address the call to action with renewed vigor and confidence that they are in the right place at the right time and what they do matters.

Questions and Answers

As with any audience involvement included in the body of your talk, make sure you have arranged for a microphone and ask that it be used when you engage in Q&A. Even then, it is wise to repeat the questions, especially when the session is being recorded.

Q&A is often where a speaker shines, and yet it can take enormous skill and resiliency. What if there are no questions? You might say, "I'm often asked . . ." What if you don't know the answer to a question? It's OK to say, "I don't know" or "What are *you* thinking about that question?" What if someone attacks you verbally? First, recognize any physical constriction you experience as a signal to make a mindful choice about your response. For example, if you feel your lips tightening, relax your mouth to take you into an internal place of acceptance. If your breathing becomes restricted, take a moment to calm yourself with a conscious breath. Remind yourself to be curious rather than allow yourself to be drawn into trying to win an argument. Possible replies include these suggested by Angeles Arrien: "That is the first time I've received this feedback. I will consider it," or, if it has merit, "I have heard that before and am addressing it. I apparently still have some work to do in that regard."

We don't have to have all the answers. As transformational speakers, our role is to stimulate dialogue and creative thinking. Creativity comes not from conformity but from diversity. Our differences provide the stimulation to stretch and expand us.

One of the most beautiful moments I ever saw was when presidential candidate Dennis Kucinich took his campaign to the Santa Fe High School Auditorium. The entire time he spoke, a large woman dressed in a bright red suit and matching hat was hollering incoherent responses to what he said and generally annoying the crowd. When Dennis asked for questions, he went down to the floor level to speak with people. Here she came, yelling at the top of her lungs as she lunged down through the bleachers to get to the floor. Kucinich met her halfway and held the microphone to her mouth as she screamed about the dangers of radioactivity at Los Alamos National Laboratory and the poisoning of the land and groundwater. She had a good point but a challenging way of presenting it. Still, he listened carefully. After several minutes, he gently and reassuringly put his hand on her arm. With this positive reassurance that her views had been heard and acknowledged, she ran out of steam. Rather than responding to her directly, Dennis turned to the audience and said, "We must listen to this woman. She is a voice for Mother Earth."

Eleanor Roosevelt said, "The giving of love is an education in itself." Dennis chose not to meet resistance head-on and instead displayed curiosity and compassion—indeed, love—so he could hear the message underneath the angry delivery. A challenging situation dissolved and a man small in physical size achieved presidential stature in a healing moment that was witnessed by all.

The Use of Quotations and the Work of Others

Stirring quotations reinforce our beliefs and illuminate our points. However, use them only to support your own original thinking or you'll simply be a repository of other people's work. As one participant in a Real Speaking class said, "We should be quoting ourselves. We're good!" The playwright George Bernard Shaw voiced the same sentiment when he said, "I often quote myself. It adds spice to my conversation."

A colleague once asked me to join her to listen to a woman she admired speak about holistic health. After the presentation, my friend asked, "Wasn't she great?!"

"She's a really good speaker technically," I responded, "but I doubt she'll go far."

"Why not?"

"Because she gave a brilliant account of what Deepak Chopra, Larry Dossey, and Bernie Siegel have already written about. I didn't hear one original word that expressed her own point of view or story."

Your speaking is about your perspective. Never let the great work of others usurp your own. And when you use poetry or quotations to support your point of view, take the time to memorize them so they become a seamless part of your presentation. People often tell me, "I can't memorize the way you do." I was inspired by Angeles Arrien's capacity to quote vast amounts of poetry and at first found it impossible to remember the lines I wanted to learn until I gave myself permission to learn only one line a day. By adding the next line each day, I not only gave myself space, but I also picked up my pace.

The Gift of Humor

In professional speaking it is said, "You don't have to be funny to speak, only to get paid for it." Humor is a wonderful gift, representing the shortest distance between two people. When we are able to laugh together, barriers dissolve and good things begin to happen.

If you're funny in real life, humor can't help but enter into your speaking. If you're the life of the party, you will show up as such on stage. If you're dry and deadpan, you can rely on understatement working for you when you're in front of an audience.

If you're not funny, work on lightening up. Allow yourself to laugh, especially at yourself. Expose the ridiculous in your life to a trusted friend and see what happens. A friend of mine who had been desperately depressed told me of his futile suicide attempts. Once he dressed in black and planned to hurl himself onto a busy freeway in the dark of night, forgetting about all the overhead freeway lights. So he went home. The next time he planned to drown himself in a canal and arrived on a night the city drained it of water. At that point, he started to think the Mystery might have another plan for his life. We howled with laughter—in retrospect, of course.

Madame Ovary was born of the most humiliating experience of my life, a story I didn't tell anyone for nearly two years. When I did tell it, feeling vulnerable and shamed, my friend Adrienne laughed so hard the tears were running down her face. "This isn't funny!" I exclaimed in anger. "It's the funniest thing I ever heard!" she replied. "Write about it—but write funny." That moment shape-shifted my entire experience and launched a new story that became a book and a festive presentation, and, most of all, allowed me to view midlife as an art form. Now that was a great new story! Here is the experience I shared with Adrienne that launched several thousand bucks (per speech):

The Skinny on Liposuction
by Madame Ovary®

A defining moment of truth alerts us to the inevitable fact that we are aging. You'd think it would come *before* a person decides on plastic surgery and in fact provide the impetus for such an extreme act. Not so for me. Mine came as a *result* of plastic surgery.

It all started when I entered a dress shop and the sales associate asked, "Can I help y'all?" I was alone, and I was not in the South. Until then I thought I was doing a pretty good job of concealing my expanding girth by adopting the "goddess" look: flowing dresses and skirts with long overblouses that hid a lot of denial. But now I had to face the truth I'd been dressing in the dark for two years to avoid: It was time to cut out the fat. And in this day and time, it's possible to have a surgeon do that for you.

I consulted with three doctors and several satisfied patients before deciding on liposuction. "Lipo," as it is referred to by the initiated, involves a surgeon vacuuming out the fat cells just beneath the skin in areas of the body that torment you the most. Never having even pierced my ears because in New England, where I grew up, only floozies engaged in such scandalous self-mutilation, suddenly I was planning to puncture my body from my navel to my thighs. This was clearly the act of a desperate woman. I never told my mother.

They'll tell you the pain of lipo is like the muscle ache from strenuous exercise. (This should arouse your suspicion. If you knew what strenuous exercise felt like, would you be here?) They'll also tell you that you can resume exercise a few weeks following surgery. (I guess you could call it that if your idea of resuming exercise consists of regaining sufficient muscle control to land on the toilet from a one- instead of a three-foot drop.)

Armed with this useless orientation, I planned for what I felt was the worst-case scenario, based on my low tolerance for pain. I anticipated up to five days in bed, followed by several weeks of wearing the requisite girdle contraption to aid the healing. Then I expected to resume life, feeling and looking a bit better each day. Right.

My first mistake was in failing to check out, *before* surgery, the girdle I would be required to wear in the aftermath. I'd heartily recommend not just looking at it but trying it on. Consider that it encases you from just below your breasts to your knees. Then imagine yourself trapped in this for six weeks, removing it only to shower and only then with the help of one or more of your most supportive friends. Then consider, when you are finally permitted to take it off, thinking it has been the source of your ongoing pain and discomfort, you will voluntarily put it back on because it feels so good. In short, you will have a codependent relationship with this garment. Get used to it.

My second mistake was in extremely poor planning. It took five weeks to even attempt a walk, an activity I undertook solely out of compassion for my dachshund puppy Sienna, who was missing her morning ritual. Wearing a sweat suit over my "requisite undergarment," I progressed a very slow block and a half, but at least I was moving. It could have been the beginning of my new exercise regime, but not today.

Two six-year-olds waiting for the school bus had talked their adult companion into letting them bring along their two sixty-pound bulldogs, their retractable leashes held loosely by the children's sides. At the first sight of Sienna, they were off. Sienna was terrified, and where I ordinarily could have picked her up, I was immobilized by the undergarment and unable to bend over. The adult yelled at one of the kids to hold on to a leash he had retrieved while he went after the second bulldog. The kid held on all right, and the retractable leash wound around my legs as the bulldog chased Sienna around and around, eventually knocking me over like a felled tree.

A small crowd of onlookers gathered to view the spectacle of an apparently inflexible woman laid out in the street, unbent by the trauma. One man leapt from his car and, handing me his card, yelled, "I saw everything!" I did not find this comment reassuring. Fortunately his humanity ultimately outweighed his ability to sniff out a potential legal proceeding and he offered me a ride home. I was sufficiently protected by shock not to recall how I got in and out of his car, which I must have accomplished while clutching my dog.

Within minutes of my arrival home, the bulldogs' owner heard the story and came to check on me. A man only a few years my junior, he apologized profusely, telling me how angry he was that his friend let the children hold the dogs' leashes. "A child can't hold back sixty pounds," he fumed. "I told him a fall is bad enough, but for an older person like you . . ."

So much for recapturing my lost youth. But it doesn't matter. I will never leave home again.

Telling jokes is a poor substitute for sharing the richness of living. Nothing is funnier or more poignant than our real-life experiences. Our desperation strikes a special chord because it helps others laugh about the human condition and see themselves in a new light for feeling the same things. As Madame Ovary has discovered, sharing the unspeakable opens the door to conversations that need to happen, and humor is often the key.

Creating Intimacy

It is an axiom of public speaking that although an audience may not remember what you said, they'll remember how you made them feel. They'll remember you even more when you feel with them. Feelings and presence have their own language, as Nicole Sedgwick Stewart, a social entrepreneur and Isagenix International distributor from Vancouver, British Columbia, discovered when traveling to Taiwan to give a presentation. Nicole's mission is to make a profound difference in the life of women and children around the world and create global oneness through honoring diversity. She is learning Mandarin with the help of a tutor and included her five-year-old daughter, Ashley, in the lessons. Ashley also learned a children's song, which she patiently taught to her mom. While most of Nicole's presentation was in English and communicated through an interpreter, her energy is what won over her audience. She began her speech in the Mandarin language and shared the song she had learned as the audience joined in. The response she received was over the top from people who felt her love and commitment to their culture and responded in kind. Nicole explained, "I found my words didn't matter nearly as much as revealing who I am." She honored her audience by greeting them in their own language and illuminated an essential aspect of her own medicine of joyful and heartfelt connection with others.

In addition to telling your story from a heartfelt place, there are three things you can do to invite the audience to connect with you. One is to be specific rather than to generalize. For example, if you refer to a significant story in the midst of a speech, tell it. You can't just mention you're trying to overcome a bad habit; come out and tell us you're struggling with your addiction to shopping or television news or your daily latte. If you don't, your audience gets left behind in wondering about the unspoken, or worse, thinks you are hiding something. Conversely, if you know there is a negative story circulating about you or you've been the subject of unflattering public speculation, it is better to address and diffuse it rather than hope it will go away.

A second way to create intimacy is to claim your own experience rather than assume others feel the same way. It's a common speech pattern to say, "When you're up against something like that, you . . ." rather than "When I found myself in that position, I . . ." The latter is stronger and more direct.

It is also important to include yourself in the collective human experience rather than act like you've somehow managed to escape it. The use of "we" instead of "you" when describing a problem or proposing a solution indicates you include yourself in the need for change.

Know Where You Are Going

As you consider which elements to include in your presentation, you must have absolute clarity about where you are going so your audience can go with you. When you know your core message, the life experience from which it originated, your key points and the material that best supports them, the better story you'd like to see your audience embrace, and your call to action, you can eliminate the details and departures that take you and your audience off track. Eliminate the unnecessary so the necessary can be heard. The wise counsel of Antoine de Saint-Exupéry sums it up: "Perfection is not when there is no more to add, but no more to take away."

"Rough Draft" Rehearsal

Once you have a format you like, run through it once or twice aloud to see how it holds together and to time it. Next step, unless you're tweaking a speech you've given successfully before, is to gather your friends and colleagues for a rehearsal. Invite people with different perspectives, such as intuitive and intellectual, who are likely to hear in the diverse ways your audience might. If you haven't yet trained your associates in the art of gentle feedback, create a structure to receive their comments in the way you want to hear them.

Questions you might ask include the following: What stands out? Where were you excited? Where were you apprehensive? Was anything unclear? What might you do differently as a result of my talk? Have you heard this before? If so, was there something original about the way I said it? Have my best personal qualities been revealed in the way I'm doing it?

I never launch a new program without inviting at least one person to hear my "rough draft." I, too, hear it in a different way when I speak to my mini-audience of well-trained critics. If it's fabulous, I merely tweak it. If it flops, I go back to the drawing board. But when I step up to the platform, as we'll discuss in the next chapter, I'm confident I have a structure that will work.

8

Show Time!

Taking the Stage

Committing to a speaking engagement, if done wisely, is much more than readily agreeing to a time and a topic. Many speakers just show up, take what's offered, and hope for the best. That is neither necessary nor advisable. All presenters—but transformational speakers especially—require a clear picture of the overall program and the venue so they can ask for what they need well in advance. Preparing adequately and making adjustments as necessary will make all the difference in your comfort level and ultimate success. Let's take a look at what you can do to ensure that the environment, both without and within, supports you in giving your best.

Outer Space: Attending to What Surrounds You

Speaker preferences vary, and one size does not fit all. Once you know what works for you, commit it to writing as a set of instructions you include with the letter of agreement when you accept an engagement. (See Resouces for what to include in your letter of agreement.) Key areas to anticipate, understand, and, if necessary, negotiate are the program, the venue, and the equipment.

The Program

In addition to confirming the time you are scheduled to speak, ask your on-site contact what is planned in the room both before and after your presentation. Arrange time before the program to check the room setup and microphone. Find out whether the room is available after your presentation to continue conversation with audience members or, if you are an author, to sign and sell books. If the room is unavailable, ask whether you can move to another location and, before your talk ends, let people know where you'll be. Even if the room is available, respect the event schedule by sticking to the time allotted for your formal presentation.

If a meal is being served, request of the organizers that servers stay off the floor during your presentation. As you've likely observed even at your own dinner table, people are typically more interested in mastication than illumination. Remember Maslow's hierarchy of needs? The worst tiramisu can upstage the best speaker! It is customary to wait until dessert and coffee have been served before introducing a key speaker. Insist on this courtesy if you're speaking at a lunch or dinner function.

The Venue

The way you set up your space will either support or diminish your capacity to be a transformational speaker. Ask your host to describe the room, the size and height of the stage or platform (or riser) if there is one, and the planned seating arrangements. If the venue does not provide the best environment for the experience you wish to create for your audience, ask for what you need. If adjustments are not forthcoming, consider how you yourself can alter the space, and arrive early enough to do so. For example, if you are asked to speak from a high stage and you want to move to the floor or walk down the center aisle, you'll need to ensure that there is an easy way down from the front of the stage.

Speaking from a stage with a microphone is not necessarily the best setup. Many speakers prefer to address smaller groups seated in a circle to create a sense of intimacy. Retreat centers, generally more casual than hotels, will find this request typical. In fact, you may have to ask for actual chairs instead of back-jacks or cushions! (If your audience will include aging boomers, whose numbers are legion, or their elders, be kind: provide chairs.) At a hotel, you may have to arrange the seating yourself because meeting rooms are typically arranged for the "sage on the stage" model. Craig Neal, creator of the Art of Convening trainings and Heartland, Inc., who arranges his settings so that people can connect more deeply with their purpose and vision, often rents country clubs for events. The pricing is good, the setup options are numerous, and the natural setting is conducive to deep work.

"Meeting technology is manipulative and typically hierarchical," Craig observes. "In reality, people want to gather in an essential way." As in the World Café process, originated by Juanita Brown and David Isaacs and described in their book by the same title, where small groups of people move from table to table to discuss ideas and seed new possibilities, Craig uses "circle technology" no matter what the group size is. When hired to work with 350 bankers in Minneapolis, he and his partner divided the group into two, arranging 175 chairs in three rows around a focal point in the center of each. His intention in using the circle setup is to create an environment where everyone can see one another; like the campfire, there is a natural sense of connectedness and collegiality. I asked whether clients ever got nervous about this setup. "If I were self-conscious, they'd be self-conscious," Craig explained. "The more I have my stake in the ground, the better it works." Let his confidence about what best supports his approach inspire you to ask for what you need.

Dead Space Kills Speeches: Ideally, unless you are planning a circle, you want a room that doesn't have quite enough seating. A full house is exciting for everyone. That said, make sure there are more chairs on hand. One of my clients had two choices of venue for his book launch. One space was a large restaurant that could accommodate more than a hundred people. The other was a studio where perhaps twenty could sit in chairs and the rest would sit on pillows or stand. Knowing he would have at least thirty people but well below a hundred, I recommended the studio. About fifty people came and we crowded in, setting the intimate conversational space that was just right for this speaker. During the Q&A following his presentation, a voice shouted, "You can't see me because I'm standing in the bathroom, but I have a question!" It was a memorable and wildly successful evening. In a half-empty restaurant, it could have felt like a bust.

Similarly cavernous space between the speaker and the audience is lethal to group dynamics. If a hotel meeting room is too large for the size of the audience, staff will often leave ten to twenty feet of empty, energy-sucking space between the speaker and the first row to balance the room. I ask that the front row or table be no more than five feet from the speaking platform or place in the room where I will deliver my talk. Bridging physical distance to reach your audience detracts from creating connection with them.

Staging: Meeting rooms are usually set for more than the number expected to accommodate late registrants. This works well for opening keynote speeches and general sessions. However, it disperses the energy of smaller groups such as those attending break-out sessions or the closing keynote. If you anticipate that the group will be small and see that the stage or riser is too high, ask in advance that the lectern be moved to floor level. You want to be on level with a small audience, not above them. The back rows can be cordoned off to move people up front, or you can invite people to move up. Often you will have to take charge in the moment to create a situation that works for you.

For example, scheduled to present a 4:00 PM workshop at the Business of Healing Conference in Joshua Tree, California, I could see I would face problems. I was programmed in the main hall that Dan Millman, best-selling author of *Way of the Peaceful Warrior,* had filled with his keynote the night before. I knew my audience would be much smaller than Dan's. In fact, I wondered whether there would be any audience at all given that two sessions were scheduled at the same time as mine and it was a beautiful day that beckoned people outdoors. To complicate the situation, the planned 2:30 PM break had been eaten up because the speaker before me ran over her time. As I thought about my upcoming talk, I took a walk for a cup of tea and felt revitalized by the cool March breeze and warm sunshine. When I returned at 3:45, the previous speaker was taking questions, and at 3:50 I said I needed the space.

I had presented a successful general session that morning and many people had said they were looking forward to my workshop. As for me, I stood at the front of that room and was feeling pretty depleted until I noticed a beautiful side patio in the sunshine that was calling my name. I checked my idea out with the people who had arrived for my workshop and told the audio/visual tech that I was moving outside. He said being outside would compromise the videotaping. I said I'd much rather have a fabulous session with a lousy videotape than a lousy session with a fabulous videotape. Everything turned out fine, and my group grew as people walked by and saw what the sun and I had to offer. Don't be afraid to wing it and remove yourself from the organizer's comfort zone to your home zone. In this case, my home zone was the patio.

The Looming Lectern: The lectern is both literally and figuratively friend or foe. Hotels often have a big ole honkin' lectern, sometimes called a podium, sporting their logo, placed smack in the middle of the stage. Most speakers take great care in choosing a fabulous outfit for the occasion. Well, standing behind the looming lectern you may as well be naked. No one will see anything but your head and possibly shoulders. Most lecterns would dwarf Paul Bunyan.

Lecterns are for those who need something to hold on to or who plan to read their speeches. By now, your speech is such a part of you that you are not reading it. If you want or need your notes, your storyboard should be down to a few pages of sticky-notes or a typed outline. Put your pages in a thin three-ring notebook so they won't fly away in a strong breeze or be carried off by your introducer. Then ask for the lectern to be placed toward one side of the speaking area, angled toward you. You can stand next to it if you want something to rest a hand on. Never stand behind it. If it is off to the side, you can walk by and glance at your notes when needed.

Water: Have a room-temperature glass of water at hand. Avoid ice water because it constricts your vocal cords. There's usually a shelf inside the lectern where you can place it.

Equipment

Microphone: I prefer a wireless lapel mike that leaves my hands free. If you go this route, make sure you're not wearing jewelry that may rub against it and distort the sound. The receiver is in a small box that attaches to your belt or waistband, so dress accordingly. The on/off switch is on the box. Once it is on, be aware that everyone can hear you. It is bad form to have a private conversation or, worse, go the restroom once you're "on." Ask the tech to show you the on/off switch and don't turn it on until you are being introduced.

Handheld microphones can be wireless or have a cord. If you're stuck with the latter, make sure the cord is long enough to allow you to move around. Hold the mike an inch or so below your mouth. Be careful not to gesture with the hand holding it or people won't be able to hear you. Practice ahead of time, even with a toy "echo mike." When you hear the echo as you speak, you know you are holding it properly.

The standing mike is a pole with an attached handheld microphone you can remove and hold in your hand. If you elect not to hold it, check the height of the stand to make sure the mike is positioned correctly. Know how to adjust it before you go on stage, because the person preceding you may have set it at a different height. I recommend you hold the mike so you are free to move around and more fully inhabit your body.

Then there is the upscale "Madonna mike" that fits around your head. Although these are the most high tech, I find them uncomfortable and distracting. Unless you're a rock star doing dance numbers, avoid these annoying devices.

Well before the program begins, arrange a sound check with a technician to make sure all is working properly. If no tech is on hand, ask who knows the equipment and can meet you to test the sound.

Slide Projectors, PowerPoint, and Other Visual Equipment: A great deal has been written about the use of technology as an aid to public speaking. It isn't my specialty. In my opinion, you are your best visual. The only exception I would make is to use images that are so soul-stirring they bring your core message home in a way words cannot. Keep visuals with text to a minimum.

If you're using PowerPoint, be sure to turn it off when you aren't specifically referring to the material on the screen. Otherwise, assuming you are remembered at all, it will be for reading well, and perhaps for a smashing handout that ends up forgotten in a file. The time you spend playing with colors and fonts on your computer could be spent becoming a compelling speaker.

An example of a gripping use of film comes from a story I read about a speech by Jane Goodall at Omega's Century of the Environment Conference. She told of a scientific meeting where people who looked at wildlife as something only to be managed gathered to discuss whale behavior. A respected scientist showed for the first time a piece of film from an expedition where they came across the dead body of a large humpback. As two divers prepared to swim toward the huge carcass, another male humpback appeared and did what a mother whale does for its newborn to get it to take its first breath. He repeatedly brought the huge dead body up to the surface and held it there for a while and then let it sink down. "At last, after half an hour of this effort he circled and swam to the dead male again," Jane reported. "This time, he opened his huge pectoral fins and he simply embraced the huge, dead body. And stayed this way for about four hours."

Jane went on to say, "People in the room began analyzing and giving academic explanation for the whale's behavior. Finally the scientist who had filmed it said, 'I don't understand it, but I have entitled my video *No Greater Love*.'

"Then everybody cried," Goodall said. "Things are changing. It's happening. And we can do it not by yelling but by telling stories, by opening [our] hearts."

I cried reading the story. I can only imagine the impact of seeing it.

Whatever equipment you use, arrive early to make sure it is working properly. Nothing is more frustrating to an audience than watching a speaker fumble around with technology. That said, inevitably it will fail on occasion. When that happens, it is wise to have an alternate plan.

I once attended what I thought was a keynote speech by a prominent futurist and upon arriving learned she was going to be televised live. When we heard only her voice with no visual image, the emcee didn't know what to do. Had she been prepared with a backup plan, she could have gone to other material while the technicians struggled. Instead, we were treated to twenty minutes of live commentary between the emcee, the speaker, and the technicians. Hardly a stunning opening to a four-day conference.

Inner Space:
Calming, Centering, Preparing

Before you take the stage, the speaking platform, the microphone, or the floor, take a moment to silently state your intention for your speech and move from the machinations of your mind to whatever practice will settle and support you. You likely have your own methods. Here are others you may wish to try.

Prayer

Trusting that your preparation will serve you well, now is the time to ask for assistance from the Mystery or however you understand your higher power. Doreen Virtue, author of *Angel Therapy*, offers an effective phrase in her CD *Chakra Clearing* that is easy to remember: "I step back and let Spirit lead the way."

One client told me he wanted Spirit to move through him every time he spoke, to begin and stay in his home zone. "Do you ask for that?" I inquired. He looked perplexed as the realization dawned that asking for what he wanted would be a good thing to do. It reminded me of the song lyric "Way down yonder by myself, I didn't hear nobody pray." I don't want to feel way down yonder by myself when I'm speaking. We have much support in the unseen world, from God, the Great Spirit, to our ancestors, our angels, and our allies. However, they wait to be asked. They revel in an assignment! Develop a relationship and ask for support. Calling upon whatever lineage or spiritual beings we relate to provides a powerful sense of confidence and connectedness.

I use a practice of calling in the resource that will most support me and placing it all around me. It takes just a moment of tuning in to an internal strength such as courage, trust, serenity, humor, or clarity, and asking to be protected and surrounded by what I most need for my well-being in that moment. If I feel the group will be receptive, I often ask them to join me as a way of becoming present.

Breath

"Fear is merely excitement without the breath." So stated legendary psychiatrist Fritz Perls (as noted on page 11). When Sankara Saranam, founder of the Pranayama Institute and author of *God Without Religion*, attended Real Speaking, I asked him to develop some breathing exercises for speakers. His suggestions that follow are remarkable tools for becoming present and focused. In fact, ecopreneur Russell Precious labeled these practices ones that calm the "Cuisinart mind with time-released adrenaline, a great anti-dote to overpreparation."

Here are three simple yet highly effective methods to gain focus and use nervous energy to your benefit. These methods also can be used before meeting someone, to regain composure in a tense moment, or simply as a meditative exercise in the morning and evening. Close your eyes and direct your attention upward toward the third eye, between the eyebrows, especially with every inhalation.

1. *Tension-relaxation.* This exercise invigorates and relaxes the body. Simply perform multiple inhalations with the mouth closed while simultaneously tensing the entire body. Multiple inhalations are done by breathing in with several small, quick intakes of breath, completing with a long, full inhalation. While tensing, progressively curl the toes, tense the calf muscles, tighten the thighs, clench the fists and buttocks, tighten the abdomen, chest, and biceps, tense the neck, and scrunch the face. After the inhalation, hold the breath for three seconds and maintain the tension in the entire body. Then open the mouth and perform a double exhalation while quickly relaxing the body. To energize and heal a body part, relaxation is normally done very slowly, but to loosen all the big and small muscles, relax them very quickly. You can perform this exercise six to twelve times in a row before proceeding to the next.

2. *Square breathing.* Next, slowly inhale through the nostrils, filling the lower then upper lungs by expanding the abdomen and chest, to a count of six to twelve seconds, depending on your lung capacity. Hold the breath for the same duration, then exhale through the mouth for the same duration. Do this a dozen times. This technique naturally levels the emotions, calms the mind, and introverts the awareness. While tension-relaxation dispels restlessness, square breathing harnesses nervous energy for positive use.

3. *Multiple exhalations.* After the above exercise, chop up the exhalation and stall the inhalation to induce calm and focus. While waiting for the call to speak, exhale through the mouth with breaks, making the sound "huh, huh, huh," then end with a long "huuuuuh" until all the air is out. This is nature's way of releasing excess carbon dioxide from the body, a main reason why laughter is so therapeutic. Since you may not want to break into raucous guffaws backstage while you are being introduced, use multiple exhalations to reap the same benefit. And there's an added bonus if, after the last long exhalation, you keep the breath out for three to six seconds: it slows the heart, naturally introverts the awareness, and bestows calmness and intensity of concentration. Practice a dozen multiple exhalations, each with a few moments of breathlessness before inhaling.

If you're soft-spoken and have to rev up before you speak, use these methods to become calm and centered. Then breathe in, open your eyes wide, and envision yourself making a grand entrance. Remember, what feels grand to you is likely understated to your audience, which also rarely notices that you're nervous.

Write Your Own Introduction

The way you are introduced is essential to how you are received. Great introducers are rare; don't sabotage yourself by telling someone he can introduce you however he sees fit. You may be stuck with someone who thinks he's funny or, worse if you're a humorist, funnier than you are. Instead of leaving it to chance, let the organizer know you have composed an introduction that is essential to your presentation and ask that it be read exactly as written.

When crafting your intro, decide what adds credibility for this particular engagement and audience, and write it accordingly. Think about the mood you want to create taking the stage. It is an axiom of public speaking that "They don't care how much you know until they know how much you care," so spare your audience a recitation of all your accomplishments or they'll zone out before you step up. Less is more. Provide more detailed background information in a brochure or the event program, if possible. This should also include contact information.

Keep the intro short, sweet, wise, and wonderful. Use short sentences that are conversational. Read it aloud to make sure it sounds as good as it looks on paper. Keep reworking it until it sounds just the way you want it to and you can't wait to hear what you have to say.

Ta da! You're on. Take another deep breath. You're confident. Avoid thanking everyone from the introducer to the organizers to the volunteers to your mother to the airline pilot who got you there safely. It doesn't work, even at the Academy Awards. Move directly into your speech and the dynamite opening you've already prepared. Trust you have everything you need within you to deliver a speech that matters.

When you think a presentation will make or break you, it's time to lighten up and remember you are there to connect with the people who want you to be your best so they get what they came for. This is the time to say to yourself, "This is not about me. As a person who has something significant to share, I commit to getting out of my own way."

Now for looking the audience in the eye. Typically, there will be a person to whom you are naturally drawn because he or she is fully present and already engaged. When you first make eye contact, silently say "namaste" (pronounced nah-mah-STAY, Sanskrit for "The spirit in me honors the spirit in you") as a way of extending respect. Even though the greeting is unspoken, the other person will consciously or unconsciously register the acknowledgment. Then expand that sense of appreciation to the entire room of people. They've come to support you in what you are here to do.

With the work you've done thus far in mastering both the heart and the art of transformational speaking, you will likely be as busy as you want to be with your speaking engagements. In part 3, we will explore personal sustainability and energy dynamics so you will be able to remain whole in the work of change.

Part 3 THE **ENERGETICS** OF
TRANSFORMATIONAL
SPEAKING

**Remaining Whole
in the Work of Change**

9

Body Rules

Extreme Cherishment of Your Precious, Worthy Self

"Let us take care of the children, for they have a long way to go. Let us take care of the elders, for they have come a long way. Let us take care of those in between, for they are doing the work." This African prayer is a reminder that no matter how great a speaker you become, you need the support of a strong physical body to do your best work. Without good health, you lack the foundation to bring your gifts to the world.

This recognition comes from personal experience. Years ago when a close friend suggested I was taking on too much, I discounted it, wondering whether he were envious of my active "glamorous" life. I use the word *glamour* tongue in cheek. Excessive travel is not an adventure but a marathon. It is stressful not only to personal but also to planetary health because of the carbon impact of flying or driving from one place to another.

In May 2007, I drove from Santa Fe to Sunport, the airport in Albuquerque, looking forward to the presentation I was to give the next day in Berkeley, California, for the annual conference of Business Alliance of Local Living Economies (BALLE). Although I had returned just ten days earlier from two weeks of teaching in

British Columbia, I had added to my calendar this challenging assignment to figure out how in one hour I could introduce the essentials of Real Speaking and get a group of eighty people practicing speaking skills. I returned from BC, developed a plan and a fun new handout, and was excited about the engagement.

When I arrived at Sunport, I learned my flight was delayed for an hour. That worked for me: I could have a relaxed lunch and recover from the rush to get ready for the trip. The checkpoint line wasn't particularly long, but it was stressful because of an inflamed Homeland Security person yelling at me to "Stop right now!" and combine my bags, which I had disassembled to exhibit my liquid items, obediently packaged in containers of fewer than three ounces. I intended to put it all back together while in the screening line where I would have access to a table. As I walked on, the woman continued to shout at me. I was fumbling and mumbling, hardly in charge of my faculties. It's no wonder I'm a control freak—catch me in a bad moment and I look my age.

But the worst of it was I felt the energy drain from my body. The pressure of the earlier trip and developing a new presentation caught up with me, as did a security person who decided to search me because of the undue attention I had drawn to myself. When I suggested to him they couldn't distinguish between a terrorist and a menopausal woman, he responded, "You mean there's a difference?" After that stimulating exchange, during which none of my weapons was found, I proceeded with my one properly combined carry-on bag to the restaurant in the expectation that a healthy repast and a large dose of chocolate would revive me.

I try to take one day at a time, but on this one a bunch of them ganged up on me all at once. Lunch didn't help, and I went to the gate only to learn it would be another two-plus hours until flight time. As I attempted to settle in for the wait, my energy plummeted further. Best case, it would be another seven hours by the time I got to Oakland, rented a car, and made my way to Berkeley, where my campus housing was located some distance from where I was to park. My mind said, "You must! You are a professional! The show must go on!" But my body shouted back, "No way!" This time, the body got to rule.

I "luv" Southwest Airlines and they earned my further admiration by locating my checked suitcase by the time I got to baggage claim. I arrived back in Santa Fe five hours after I had left home and went to bed—for three days.

This was the first speaking engagement I ever had to cancel. (I received no word that the conference suffered excessively from my absence.) Earlier in my work life, I thought I could do it all and considered speakers with demands high-maintenance. Now I remind myself—with guidelines attached to my computer—that sustained stress over time takes us down.

The body does rule. It is amazing how it generally works and supports us, but only to a point, and then it lets us know that enough is enough. Whether with adrenal exhaustion, chronic fatigue, or another stress-induced illness, our bodies find creative ways to say, "Hi, there. Remember me?" What's more, given that the first symptom of heart disease in a third of the cases is sudden death, health is not something to be taken for granted.

While I was taking my long summer's nap, I received a voice message from a friend. I had emailed her to ask whether I might stay with her while attending a conference. She expressed sheer delight that she had reached my voicemail instead of me so she didn't have to have one more conversation. As for my request to stay at her home, she said she "could not get in touch with a yes" due to "drastic overinteraction." She explained she needed to be fiercely protective of her time and space to be personally sustainable and suggested I come in a day early for the conference for quality time together and then move to a hotel.

As I listened to her message, I found myself celebrating. She trusted me to understand her need for self-care, and how could I not, prostrate as I was?

According to the U.S. Centers for Disease Control and Prevention, 75 percent of the health problems presented to medical doctors in the United States are stress related. Fighting what *is*, whether injustice or our individual realities, creates stress. We add to it when we get busy and don't exercise or eat well, telling ourselves they can wait. We fly across times zones and go directly to work, robbing ourselves of time to feel our feet on the earth and connect to something more enduring than our busy schedules and commitments. If we see an opportunity to fit in another speaking engagement and can work out the travel arrangements, we add it to an already packed schedule—unless we have body rules.

I began 2007 with a commitment to self-care. Yet the words *self-care,* it turned out, represented yet another job on my action plan and failed to inspire me. Then, at a Real Speaking graduate reunion, we explored what I call "luscious language" for the things we want most in our lives, words that rouse us to support our biggest dreams.

In declining my request to stay at her home, my friend was demonstrating what I now call "extreme cherishment of your precious, worthy self." When I say it, I become the little girl in me who knows she deserves sacred care as well as the adult who honors that need. Still, every time I type the word "precious," I have one of those God-said-"Ha!" moments because I inadvertently type "precious" with "v" instead of "c," changing it to "previous." This typo reminds me that if I don't practice extreme cherishment, my capacity for wholeness becomes but a distant memory.

Honoring the need to replenish my flagging adrenals made me aware that extreme cherishment starts with the body—indeed, the body rules! As an example of how thoughtful guidelines can structure and nourish our lives, here are my current personal "body rules" to support me in renewing my health while giving my best every time I step up for a program:

1. I will not teach two intensive programs back to back.
2. When clients ask me to offer Real Speaking in their city, I let them know that they will receive the best return on their investment if they come to Santa Fe or Whidbey Island, where they stay on site and enjoy lovely accommodations, a natural setting, conscious care, and privacy for breakthrough work.

If they want me and my associate to come to them, we require the same qualities in the program venue.

3. When I go out of town, for every six hours I travel, I arrive one day ahead of the scheduled program so I can experience the spirit of the place and enter my work refreshed and fully present. After the program, I stay an extra night to relax and integrate the experience before heading to the airport. (I suggest participants do the same.)

4. Because I need privacy and focus, I choose not to stay in a private home the night before a program. I request a scent- and smoke-free hotel room, preferably one where the windows open.

5. I limit air travel to one trip of not more than ten days each month.

6. I wait twenty-four hours before responding to a speaking request to make sure it represents an engagement where I can add value with a happy heart. If it requires airline travel, the opportunity or compensation must make it worth my one trip by air that month.

7. To sustain our larger body, the planet, I log on to one of the many websites that allow me to calculate and mitigate the cost of my travel to the environment by contributing to carbon offset projects. For example, to offset the impact of three roundtrips between Albuquerque and Vancouver in 2007 costs $158.51. A good source for information on addressing carbon emissions is www.carbonconcierge.com, a project of Social Venture Network and Bainbridge Graduate Institute.

Learn what works for you. Most speakers arrive a day ahead of time, not only to begin their work refreshed but also to allow for unexpected travel delays. Poet David Whyte declines social activities on that early arrival day. Sandra Ingerman trains other teachers to guide people in the shamanic work to which she is committed. International workshop leader Runa Bouius books her own hotel even when she has friends and family eager to host her. Many in-demand professional speakers accept international engagements only when the compensation includes two first-class airline tickets, combining a busy schedule with a vacation with their beloved. Others might fly the most inexpensive way possible to support a cause because they are energized by the experience.

Your own rules will emerge. Take a hint from your Myers-Briggs type (available at www.humanmetrics.com), a personality inventory based on the work of Swiss psychiatrist Carl Jung. If you're an extrovert, you get energy from others. If you're an introvert, you need time alone to regenerate. If your personality is midway between extrovert and introvert, as mine is, you must maintain an intricate balance between socialization and solitude. If you go too long without personal space, you create intolerable stress for yourself (and likely the people around you). Likewise, without sufficient stimulation, you may become despondent.

Sometimes we wonder whether we can afford to make the promises to ourselves that body rules require—after all, we have a mission!

Yet can we afford not to?

We hardly make much of a difference by dragging ourselves reluctantly from one commitment to the next, growling at those in our paths as though we were trained by Dobermans—or, conversely, staying "up" by running on adrenaline, which is easy to do when we love our work but which ultimately depletes our overall health and enthusiasm.

As you develop your own body rules, consider those below, suggested by my clients and subscribers to the Real Speaking e-letter:

When Negotiating

- Ask for the fee and arrangements you need to deliver your best work with a happy heart.

On Stage

- Drink water before speaking. Make sure it's room temperature, because cold water restricts the vocal cords. Energy moves best when you are hydrated.

Travel

- Don't schedule clients the day after you return home. Use the time to fully land, reflect on what you might do differently at your next presentation, and catch up on administration. An unscheduled day also provides a buffer if your return is delayed by weather or a late or cancelled flight.
- Have your house cleaned while you are away so you return to an orderly home.

Anytime

- Sit still and breathe. Laugh just because.
- Prune and simplify where you are spending energy wastefully. If you need to pull up the drawbridge at the end of the day to restore your body and nurture your heart, explain to loved ones you're taking care of yourself, not shutting them out.
- Allow yourself a nap. Sinking into deep rest in the middle of the day is a great teacher of surrender. Try napping in the woods: hike your heart out, eat lunch, and lie on the earth to be embraced by the Mother for a little R&R.
- Set aside one day a week when you unplug from your work world and do not drive or talk on the phone. Being outside one day a week is also restorative. Spending time with animals is regenerative as well. Remembering that human beings are not the be-all and end-all refreshes the spirit.

Relationships

- Learn to ask respectfully for what you need, without making anyone wrong.
- Negotiate when your partner wants company for an outing and you need to care for yourself by staying home.
- Learn to set boundaries even when they seem radical. Conversely, begin to acknowledge your friends and family

when they do the same. Work on negative emotions that build up between you and those around you. Speaking about your feelings while taking responsibility for them can clear the air and build trust.

Take the time now to establish your own "body rules" for the practices that work for you to manage the accumulated stress of your life. These rules will be subject to change as you continue to learn about what works best for you. Unless you are fully present and whole in what matters to you, you can't sustain the work of change.

10

Energy Awareness

Understanding and Managing Invisible Dynamics

Today there is a new conversation about energy, frequency, and vibration and the unseen dynamics that underlie every thought, communication, and interaction. When Norman Vincent Peale published *The Power of Positive Thinking* in 1952, I wonder whether he knew he was a harbinger of a message equivalent to that confirmed by quantum physics. Today's science demonstrates that nothing is separate from the one energy field that links everything and that every action and thought has an impact on the entire pulsating web of life. In fact, it has been demonstrated that the expectations of a scientist about how an experiment will turn out influences the outcome. As a speaker, your understanding of the dynamics of energy can provide a vital pillar of support for your physical and emotional well-being and your experience of speaking.

The 2007 release of the best-selling film and book *The Secret* awakened even more people to an understanding of the universe as a dynamic web of interconnection organized by the law of attraction. According to this principle, the thoughts we think literally create our world because they put out an energy frequency that attracts the same frequency. In *The Secret*, this principle was liberally applied to achieving personal prosperity, but it also applies to our health, our relationships, our life experience in general, and consequently the state of the world we see. And, of course, our speaking!

This chapter is a brief overview of aspects of every speaking engagement that we can't see visibly but that have a profound impact on the outcome. It includes basic practices to build your power as well as how to apply energy psychology to fear of speaking. But first let's take a look at how some speakers are applying this emerging understanding.

Applying the Principles of Energy Awareness to Speaking

Kelly La Sha is a dynamic young woman who excelled in and left behind a career in international marketing that garnered all the goodies of financial success, only to find they did not bring her joy. She has a gift of understanding subtle energy she had kept secret throughout her life that is her original medicine. (In fact, her birth name is Secret.) Her task now, like that of other visionary messengers who are introducing unfamiliar language or concepts, is to describe her awareness so that others can understand it. And that is why she came to Real Speaking, to decide whether she should move ahead with her book, *Liquid Mirror*, by seeing whether she could successfully speak about the knowledge she holds. Kelly is a breath of fresh air and speaks with the same clarity. This is how she explains energy:

> Quantum physics has done an excellent job explaining how everything in our world is made up of energy. Everything exists in an infinite field of wave possibilities. Furthermore, everything is connected and every particle contains the whole. We live in a holographic universe. It's like a big outstretched blanket with all the individual threads interwoven. When you move one corner of the blanket, it subtly affects the "oneness" of the entire blanket.

The veil of illusion works like the screen in the movie theater. We collectively project images onto it and then "forget" that we've done that because we get so absorbed in how "real" the story feels.

The phrase "Liquid Mirror" describes the interconnectedness of the entire field: the illusion playing out on the screen, the projector sending the image, the one watching, and the one consciousness that cocreates and holds all of it together. Although I use language of "parts" to describe this, in actuality nothing is separate because the whole is always present in the holographic oneness of all that is. You can also think of it like an individual cube of ice in a glass of water: the ice may appear separate from the water, but it's really one because it's made of the same stuff it floats in and will ultimately merge with the whole when it melts.

Kelly's simple analogies of a blanket, a movie theater, and an ice cube demonstrate how to speak about a concept to make it accessible to others. If we don't explain our internal experiences in a way others can understand, we are liable to be discounted as "flakes" or "woo-woo." Such labels are evidence that we either haven't been able to put into words what we're about so others can hear us, or that our audience doesn't value our inner and intuitive experience.

As speakers, we are frequently challenged to put words around our emerging comprehension of our individual roles in shaping both the larger world and how we see and experience it. A little knowledge can be a dangerous thing, and speakers should take care to use their perceptions responsibly. Human rights activist and poet Carolyn Forché experienced the opposite when she attended a hospital-sponsored event for breast cancer survivors. She was shocked when the "inspirational" speaker strutted back and forth across the stage and told the women in attendance their cancer was a result of their negative thinking. In other words, she was telling them they were to blame for their illness because they created an energetic field that attracted breast cancer into their experience.

Had I been in that audience, I would have been open to learning how to work with my subconscious mind to promote healing. I would have wanted to glean practical steps to manage stress and avoid toxicity in my food and my environment. I would have wanted to hear from someone who had been down the same road I had and could relate to the fear I felt. But the last thing I would have wanted is to have my illness used as a battering ram in an effort to elevate my awareness. This speaker's application of the concept that we create our own reality was thoughtless and inexcusable. No wonder many people think such ideas are a bunch of New Age hooey. Humans are here to grow and evolve through life lessons designed to support our development. Life is hard enough at times without a speaker suggesting the human condition is a self-imposed foible.

On the other end of the spectrum is Pasha Hogan, a young survivor, whose Creative Recovery programs inspire and empower women with breast cancer to apply their internal resources to live their lives to the fullest. An hour or a weekend with Pasha, for whom it took a third recurrence and a full mastectomy to realize she needed to change her thinking and her life, is spirited time devoted to helping women summon their personal power in support of wholeness.

Similarly, Pam Hale Tracta, author of *Flying Lessons*, shares her experience of earning her pilot's license to encourage women to go beyond survival from cancer and claim their capacity to soar no matter what. I had the opportunity to coach her in a workshop right around the time she and her literary agent were discussing whether she should publicly mention that she no longer flies solo. Pam said the coaching helped her see "it's much more authentic and helpful to those seeking maturity to admit to and, in fact, embrace new priorities and limits that come up rather than muscling through to try to prove something." (She also said she no longer smiles when she talks about her cancer: "Your coaching took me back to another time when I did that. I was thirteen and wanted to belong and decided I would smile at everyone in order to be popular. I'm letting that one go.")

Pasha and Pam have both been called to a hero's journey and are applying their stories with integrity and high regard for our tender shared humanity. Rumi said, "Let the beauty you love be what you do." These women are strong voices for beauty and strength, born of their life experience. The fact that they both have survived is a tribute to the wisdom they gained by doing the challenging inner work of consciously managing the energetic fields that impacted their health. You can apply what they learned to create a supportive speaking environment.

Energy Awareness in the Speaking Environment

Consider what happens when you walk into a room. If there's enthusiasm or conflict, you know it. If there is a negative undercurrent, it's palpable. If a conversation suddenly stops, you know you weren't expected. You're aware very quickly whether you want to be there or not by whether you feel enlivened, drained, or neutral.

As a speaker, it is essential to recognize that with each venue you step into a different energy field. Transformational speaking requires that we become consciously aware of these invisible forces and learn to deflect or manage their impact. Consider the following phrases:

I felt drained by speaking to that group.

It was like talking to a brick wall.

That conversation had me tied up in knots.

I think she's stringing me along.

I felt like he kicked me in the gut.

Or conversely:

My heart just opened up to them.

There aren't any strings attached.

I felt uplifted by being there.

He's not hiding a thing.

She was a breath of fresh air.

Energy is both invisible and potent. When you commit to a speaking engagement, the energetic undertone of both the venue and the audience is yet to be discovered. You may get an inkling of it in advance, which can help you prepare. No matter how much or how little you know about an upcoming program, tune in to how your body responds to the prospect of it. Do you feel open and engaged, or do you draw back and experience tension, perhaps apprehensive about something you can't yet put your finger on? In the best of all worlds, you can decline or remove yourself from unsupportive engagements, or use the clearing practices described later in this chapter to shift the energy. Other times you won't know what you're "up against" until you enter the room.

Discerning and addressing energy dynamics is a skill to be mastered. In a world quick to label the unseen as irrelevant or even nonexistent, this is no small assignment. However, as we increase our capacity to recognize the invisible components of any interaction, we will learn to track their impact and respond accordingly.

Sustaining Power: Personal Energy Protection

Whether you are an individual navigating a world of differences or a speaker putting yourself in front of a group, having an awareness of how the unseen dynamics of a situation or group affects you is crucial to maintaining your power and avoiding depletion. People who easily agree with you may be needy. Others may disagree and you run the risk of absorbing their resistance. These interactions can create a connecting "cord," especially if you have an attachment to a specific outcome or if it triggers a personal issue. Thoughts, too, have an effect; each one we transmit or receive lands, which is why shamanic teacher and author Sandra Ingerman recommends silently saying "Do not send" when we have a negative thought about someone.

Learning how energy impacts you requires an appreciation of your own sensitivities. Once you identify where you're losing power, you can regain it. Chapter 1 contains seven questions posed by Dr. Judith Orloff to determine whether you are an "intuitive empath." One "yes" answer means you're experiencing some difficulty; six suggest your energy is likely severely compromised.

At a class of twelve at Hollyhock Retreat Centre, Suzan was the last to speak on the first morning of the class, having listened with an open heart to the other eleven participants. When it was her turn, she was shaking. "This is what happens," she explained. "I get so frightened." In that moment, I was aware of another factor I sensed was having an effect on her, which was her openness and sensitivity to the group. I asked whether it might be the emotional impact of the personal sharing of others that could be causing her physical response. As she considered this, she realized that what she had been interpreting as fear was actually high sensitivity. With this new understanding, that night she joyfully stood up in front of fifty people and shared what she had learned about herself that had been stopping her from speaking out.

Managing energy—your own and whatever you confront—is a huge source of personal power. The practices and resources below have been valuable to me as I explore energy management in support of my own health.

Centering or Grounding

You walk onto a stage, having prepared your presentation and attended to the details of the space and your appearance. In the excitement of the moment, you may have forgotten the rest of your "groundwork": sending your awareness into your feet and down into the earth so you won't be completely in your head and easily knocked off balance, literally or figuratively.

The following exercise can help you become aware of when you are centered, or grounded, and when you are not. Have a partner about your same size stand behind you with her arms around your hips prepared to lift you ever so slightly. Think about your presentation, noting any feelings of anxiety that could take you off-center. While you do so, have your partner lift you up. This is no weight-lifting feat but rather a way for you to experience the physical sensation of residing primarily in your head.

Then firmly plant your feet on the ground and sink into your center, bending your knees slightly if it feels better. Breathe into your belly and find an image that helps you reach deep into the heart of the earth to connect to its strength. I like to think of a tree trunk. Others envision a cord of light or a rope tethered to the ground. Once your posture and image are in place, ask your partner to try to lift you again. You will likely be immovable.

Centering before you go on to speak is key to maintaining and balancing your personal energy and power. Make this exercise a part of your preparation.

While doing the exercise above, were you able to feel your feet by bringing attention to them? Roberta Meilleur, the inspirational creator of World Dance, teaches movement by asking participants to work with isolated parts of the body. For example, below are ways to become aware of your basic support, the feet:

1. Feel where the weight normally falls in your feet (front? back? sides?) and then experience the weight in center as true balance.
2. Putting your weight on your heels, tap the toes of both feet on the floor.
3. Switch your weight to your toes and tap both heels on the floor.
4. Pivot by alternating weight in the heels, then toes, and move sideways.
5. Put all your weight on one foot to free the other foot to shuffle, tap, touch, or kick.

6. Put all your weight on the other foot and touch the free foot to the floor with the heel, the toe, then flat-footed.

You also can bring awareness to your feet by massaging them, walking barefoot outdoors, and maintaining your focus on them as your foundation for walking in the world. Give gratitude to your lowly, fabulous feet! This will give your mind something far more productive to do than obsess about your presentation. Now is the time to trust that when you stay grounded your body remembers what your mind may no longer recall.

Chakra Clearing

A time-honored energy practice is that of clearing the energy centers of the body, called chakras. From the Sanskrit word for "wheel," chakras are invisible spinning wheels of light in the etheric body, which is the first or lowest layer in the human energy field or aura and is in immediate contact with the physical body. There are seven basic energy centers that are most commonly recognized, aligned in an ascending column from the base of the spine to the top of the head. Each chakra relates to a specific energy and is associated with a specific color. For example, the heart chakra relates to feelings of love and compassion, and the throat chakra, communication and expression. Here are the chakras in ascending order:

Chakra 1: Root chakra, located at the base of the spine, is associated with the color red. This is the grounding energy, where we connect to earth energies and tribal or family values.

Chakra 2: Sacral chakra, located just above the root chakra, is associated with the color orange. This is the energy of creativity, where we manifest ideas and balance relationships.

Chakra 3: Solar plexus chakra, located at the naval, is associated with the color yellow. This is the energy of personal power, where we develop self-esteem and make intuitive decisions.

Chakra 4: Heart chakra, located in the center of the chest, is associated with the color green or pink. This is the love center of our being, where we hold our most powerful emotions.

Chakra 5: Throat chakra, located in the throat region, is associated with the color blue. This center is the energy of communication, where we are challenged to give voice to our truth.

Chakra 6: Brow, or third-eye, chakra, located in the center of the forehead, is associated with the color indigo. This center holds the energy of vision and insight, where we develop intuitive wisdom.

Chakra 7: Crown chakra, located on the top of the head, is associated with the color violet or pure white light. This energy center connects us with our spiritual nature, where we open to our higher power and universal potential.

Your assignment is to keep them clear of the negative energy that prevents you from being available to all of who you are. To do so, I frequently use Doreen Virtue's CD *Chakra Clearing* before leaving for a speaking engagement, understanding that my most valuable work comes from clearing my energy field so that the best I have within me can be revealed with ease. Alternatively, Alberto Villoldo, referred to in chapter 4, suggests that each time you shower, you place one hand in front of each chakra, moving up from the base, and rotate your fingers counterclockwise as you envision the washing away of any old or stuck energy. Once you do this, close your energy centers one by one by rotating your fingers clockwise. Instant energy hygiene at your fingertips!

Shielding/Protection

Speakers often move quickly from one environment to another, such as from an airport to a meeting venue, then on to a social event, and finally to an unfamiliar hotel room. In each place you go to, you are unconsciously absorbing the environment into your body, especially if you are a highly sensitive person or an intuitive empath. There are practices to shield you from that which is not supportive.

The best protection of all is to keep your energy high with practices such as being in nature away from electromagnetic fields, conscious breathing, qigong, yoga, and chanting. Another widespread method is to shield yourself with protective light. Different people suggest different colors. For example, Doreen Virtue recommends imagining yourself encased in pink in the shape of a lipstick tube, pink because it radiates heart energy and deflects unwanted influences. I suggest you choose a color that delights you and makes you feel safe.

José Stevens, author of *The Power Path*, suggests imagining a rose at the edge of your energy field, no more than two to three feet from your body. Make it so beautiful you can practically smell it! You can then ask it to attract and absorb all energy that may be harmful or negative to you.

Creating Sacred Space

Begin with offering a prayer for yourself and for your audience to whomever and wherever you find inner strength and support. Whether you call on God, Great Spirit, the Universe, All That Is, the angels, or other allies in the unseen world, you can ask that you and all who enter be surrounded by protective light. In my study with Doreen Virtue, I found powerful allies in the archangels. I ask Archangel Michael to use his mighty sword to cut away anything that does not serve the highest good of all. Archangel Uriel fills the room with light. Archangel Raphael brings healing energy. Archangel Gabriel brings forth the voice of truth and heralds new life.

You can also surround yourself with an image of a symbol that has significance to you, such as a cross, placing it in each direction. Shamanic practitioners call on the four or six directions to create sacred space. The indigenous practice of using sage to smudge, or clear, a space should be done well in advance so the air is clear for those who are sensitive to smoke or aroma. You can simply light an unscented candle or place an object that has special meaning to you on the lectern. The world of Spirit stands ready to support your requests but will not interfere. That means you have to ask!

Building this energetic field supports you at all times, not only when you are speaking or anticipate a stressful situation. When you're with wonderful people who love you and blast your heart wide open, your energy field will expand. That is not the best way to go to the airport! Use these practices each day so they will support you in every interaction. You'll be healthier, and you won't be as likely to forget these tools when you enter a speaking engagement.

As energy healer and teacher Stevi Bells of Park City, Utah, asserts, "Your most important task is to build a strong energy field. The fields that make up our energy bodies, while invisible, affect us in powerful ways." There are as many as twelve layers to our energy fields, Stevi explains, extending out in all directions from our physical bodies. The most commonly recognized of these are the physical, mental, emotional, and spiritual bodies. When foreign energies penetrate the layers and attach to our energy fields, it is similar to an invasive virus or foreign object invading the body, draining our life force and leaving us feeling out of balance and often out of sorts. "When you establish and maintain your boundaries to hold your system sovereign, it is like a Teflon layer," Stevi explains. "You won't absorb what is taking place around you."

The aforementioned practices help you be aware and conscious of your energy field and assist your intention to remain clean and clear.

Using Energy Psychology to Remove Anxiety or Fear of Speaking

In her groundbreaking book *Molecules of Emotion*, Dr. Candace Pert, research professor at Georgetown University School of Medicine, explains the biochemical underpinnings that shape mood and thought. The discovery that there are receptor molecules on the surface of every cell is the foundation of the emerging field of energy psychology, which uses skin tapping and eye movement techniques to resolve negative beliefs or feelings, seemingly miraculously.

When I first witnessed these methods years ago, they seemed like hocus-pocus. But life got challenging enough to move me into an exploration of unusual healing modalities. The most helpful counsel I can provide is to try it, doubts and all. Finding something that works to alleviate your self-defeating patterns or increase your psychological and physical well-being is worth the experiment.

In the popular film *What the Bleep Do We Know?*, Candace Pert talks about the "neural pathways" that emotions and thoughts follow in the brain, often habitually. In fact, we get addicted to following familiar pathways. The work is to create new neural pathways to create a new experience by reprogramming your energy system and neurochemistry. But how?

Let's use fear of speaking as an example. You can shift your internal response to the prospect of giving a speech by employing the techniques of energy psychology. A popular modality, and one I have studied, is the Emotional Freedom Technique, referred to as EFT. (Download a free instructional handbook from www.emofree.com.) What drew me to this method is that, unlike using affirmations, it requires absolute truth telling. Affirmations, which require you to state what you want as though it already exists ("I am a confident, poised speaker") cause the skeptic in me to rail because I am being asked to withhold the truth of my experience by saying something that is not true. I suspect the use of affirmations may actually drive the offending pattern deeper and denser because it attempts to override rather than address the issue. Conversely, EFT requires that you admit to your fear with all the drama you feel about it. Use that voice. You can—and must—reveal how awful it really is for you so you can reprogram that belief. You might say, "Even though I am terrified of speaking in public and know without a doubt that I will embarrass myself so thoroughly and irreversibly that never, for all eternity, will I dare to go out in public again . . . I deeply love and accept myself." Loving and accepting yourself *as you are* is a fundamental part of the process.

As you repeat this, you'll be tapping specific points on the surface of your skin to access your energy anatomy. Some of the points used are lymphatic points where toxins can accumulate and block the flow of your body's energies. When you feel soreness at these points, it is usually because toxins are breaking apart. What you are doing is essentially opening new neural pathways.

Once the internal change takes place, it carries into your external experience. You might want to work with an EFT practitioner to find the best statement for you to support the change you want to create. Then continue the simple tapping procedure on your own as needed to reinforce the shift.

The Resources section includes references to support you as you learn to work with your energy. If this material represents a new investigation for you, I especially invite you to consider adopting just one of the aforementioned tools. Practice it daily, and observe the impact on your experience of speaking. As you do so, continually focus on your intention to radiate the positive possibilities of a new and compelling story as you claim and express your full power. Your strength becomes a part of the whole and advances the change you want to see in the world.

11

The Alchemy of Change

Choosing Power over Force

The same energetics that apply to personal wholeness play out on the larger stage when we bring our work to the world through public speaking. Our own hero's journey tells us where and to whom we are called to deliver our message. Some speakers are early voices of new ideas and confront great opposition. Others carry a message that moves people progressively to a new possibility with little resistance.

Wherever your speaking path calls you, there is power in finding the support of kindred spirits to uphold the high vibration required for the work of change. Paul Born, founder of Tamarack Institute in Ontario, Canada, which provides training and resources for building vibrant and engaged communities, offers evidence that change is ignited through the experience of a meaningful connection with others. In a Tamarack study that asked Canadians "What is your most profound experience of community?" 90 percent responded that it came from working with others to make something better.

The following statement about community offered by Starhawk, author and global justice activist, is a call to join with others to do the work that needs to be done as well as a reminder of the freedom of expression inherent in allowing ourselves to be deeply seen.

Somewhere, there are people
To whom we can speak with passion
Without having the words catch in our throats.
Somewhere a circle of hands will open to receive us,
Eyes will light up as we enter, voices will celebrate with us
Whenever we come into our own power.
Community means strength that joins our strength
To do the work that needs to be done.
Arms to hold us when we falter.
A circle of healing. A circle of friends.
Someplace where
we can be free.

When those who already resonate with who you are and what you offer become your audience, you amplify the impact of your efforts because your listeners are primed to act. For a physical analogy of this phenomenon, imagine two violins in the same room. If you pluck the G string on one instrument, the same string on the other will begin to play. This is called sympathetic resonance. All of the other strings on the violins will quiver also but to a lesser degree than the G strings, because it takes less energy to create resonance between strings with closely attuned frequencies. As a speaker, you will find people with whom you share a sympathetic vibration, and that alignment can lead to positive change.

Business consultant and executive coach Carmen Cook reports, "When I go to the first meeting with a potential client, I go with clarity and honesty to discover if the resonance that assures a successful collaboration is there. It is so rewarding to work with people who are really ready to move forward. If they're not, I've found that working with them is like eating a low-calorie meal—not sustaining!"

Alchemy was the predecessor of chemistry in its early, unscientific form, and it sought to change base metals into gold and discover a life-prolonging elixir. Similarly, today there are models of change that hold great promise for transforming our world, yet they have their share of critics. One such model is the work of David Hawkins as discussed in his book *Power vs. Force: The Hidden*

Determinants of Human Behavior. Although the applied kinesiology Hawkins used to test his results is considered pseudoscience by some, his concepts hold special relevance for transformational speakers as we decide where to commit our energies. Simply stated, our best results will come from working with audiences who are prepared to act on what we offer, thereby catalyzing both change and a higher energetic vibration that will attract more like-minded people ready to engage. Later in this chapter we will visit a model of change that parallels Hawkins's discoveries and is used to great effect in corporate settings.

When I first read *Power vs. Force*, I felt I had been thrown a life-line. I knew my work was most effective with people who have an active inner life, care deeply about the world, and are suspicious of speaking techniques that strike them as phony and manipulative. Yet I was building a business that in order to be financially viable required that I bridge my knowledge to people who are primar-ily outer-directed, or so I thought. Hawkins's work gave me a new story that changed my direction. In fact, the anatomy of my bomb in chapter 2 illustrates what happened when I applied his insights to building my business with visionary clients who welcome rather than resist my approach to speaking.

In a nutshell, here is the "better story" that Hawkins reported:

Every emotional state you experience carries with it a vibration, as discussed in chapter 10. For example, when you are depressed, your energy level carries a lower vibration than when you are feel-ing great joy. Try on the voice of depression, then the voice of joy, to experience the difference between the two in your body. Emotions such as fear, anxiety, guilt, and shame all have a low fre-quency or "vibe," while love, peace, and joy carry a high frequency or vibe. Just as emotional vibration applies to you on an individual level, it also pertains to groups of people who reside in a certain energetic range that reflects their worldview. People with a low vibe want to control others; those with a high vibe want to share who they are and help others. The higher the energetic vibration, individually or collectively, the more positive and powerful the state.

Using a vibrational scale of 1 to 1,000, Hawkins asserts that the majority of humanity, 85 percent, calibrates at a level of 207 or below. This he regards as good news, citing that in the 1980s, the world's population moved above what he calls the "Threshold of Integrity" at 200, below which are negative emotions such as shame, guilt, apathy, and fear.

Moving up the scale to the range of 300 to 400, people operate primarily from ideology. From 400 to 500, science and logic reign supreme. The next big leap in awareness is 500, where the motivation of love begins to color all activities and creativity comes into full expression. The signature of 600 is compassion and those times of illumination where duality disappears. At 700 and above is enlightenment. This level of divine grace embodies balance and harmony and includes, for example, Gandhi. The highest calibration is 1,000 and applies to those who have been called "Lord"— Lord Krishna, Lord Buddha, and Lord Jesus Christ.

Hawkins notes that higher levels can be attained with the exercise of choice and that an individual who chooses to see with the eyes of compassion, for example, can have a mighty effect. In addition, positive impact increases exponentially as we go up the scale. For example, Hawkins asserts, just one person calibrating at 700 mitigates the negative impact of 10 million people below 200. At 500, where understanding trumps judgment, one person balances 90,000 people below 200. He says, "The individual difference between a vibration of 361.0 and 361.1 is very meaningful and capable of transforming both one's life and one's effect on the world at large."

Corporate Alchemy

Applying a similar principle to organizations seeking to create and live a new story, Brian Nattrass and Mary Altomare, authors of *Dancing with the Tiger: Learning Sustainability Step by Natural Step*, work with what they call the "amoeba model of change" inspired by the work of a colleague in sustainability, Alan AtKisson. An amoeba is an amorphous single-celled organism that just can't reach out and grab hold of something it wants to ingest; it has to extend its body toward the food in a slow and deliberate process. The leading edge of the amoeba first makes contact with the food and ultimately, if the transfer is successful, the nutrient is absorbed into the body of the organism. Likewise, the global corporations with which Nattrass and Altomare work can't just grab hold of a good idea and force it into their corporate culture all at once. They must first make contact with the new idea, understand the patterns of how innovation takes hold in organizations, and then work methodically to increase the likelihood of success.

The predictable pattern of "innovation diffusion," a term coined by communications professor Everett M. Rogers in the 1960s and adopted by Nattrass and Altomare, begins with a single individual or a small group of change agents with an idea that is new to the culture. The process requires that they promote it *only* to those who are ready to "get it," people the model refers to as "early adopters." If change agents move too quickly in presenting it to skeptics, a common misstep in the fast-paced world of business, the new idea can be shot down before it has a chance to succeed. Innovation usually spreads slowly at first, but when it is successful, a critical mass is achieved and the idea takes off. As Nattrass and Altomare report, "Eventually it reaches a saturation point where everyone who is going to adopt it has done so. [Systematically] moving the idea to the point of take-off is of vital importance in any social system change initiative. If it is a good idea, it will develop a life of its own." Malcolm Gladwell applies this same concept to social issues in *The Tipping Point,* defined as "that magic moment when an idea, trend, or social behavior crosses a threshold, tips, and spreads like wildfire."

So while Hawkins's work speaks of "energetic calibration," the more mainstream approach corroborates that change occurs most efficiently when people who believe in an idea come together in support of what is possible. In the early stages, they hold close what they want to achieve, giving the idea time to take seed with others who are able to accept the new possibility. These models suggest that the key task for you as a change agent is sharing your ideas with those who understand what you're talking about and can get on board. Good ideas will take root but cannot be forced anymore than you can encourage a seed to "grow now, dammit!"

From Resistance to Resonance

Many people who have moved from a field in which they excelled to another that offers a new perspective are called to "bridge" their new awareness back to their old world. Indeed, their competence in both worlds is often what gives them the credibility to share a new story.

Yet being a bridge can be exhausting. The promise in the observations of Hawkins, Nattrass, and Altomare is that working with people who can hear us and are ready to make a shift carries much greater power than trying to appeal to those who would be quick to label us as idealistic, naive, or even threatening.

The numbers of those who resonate with your message may be larger than you think. For example, a Roper Green Gauge study found that 58 percent of people in the United States would be willing to make changes to support a healthy environment if they had specific knowledge of what to do.

Whatever your field of concern, what might you accomplish by speaking to people who are ready to make a change rather than using your energy to convince people who don't believe there is a need? By moving forward together, the power of the higher vibration pulls everything up the scale. The high vibration of joy, which Hawkins calibrates at 540 on his scale, is a real incentive to present a story that makes you happy and calls others to step up to a new possibility. Hawkins suggests that power arises from meaning and is always associated with that which supports the significance of life itself. He says, "Power appeals to what uplifts, dignifies, and ennobles." Real power comes from within; indeed, as John Trudell noted (chapter 1), "Power comes from our relationship to life."

Keep in mind that these insights are not about good versus bad or right versus wrong. They are about levels of awareness and consciously choosing where your energy can be applied for the greatest return on your investment. Which elevates your vibration—power or force? Remind yourself to use the *power* of higher values with people who can hear you rather than the *force* of argument with those who can't.

A Place for Outrage

While aligning with kindred spirits amplifies results, this is not to suggest your life and your speaking will not provide numerous outlets to express your outrage. One of my favorite television shows, no longer in production, is *Judging Amy*. Amy is a juvenile judge, and her mother, Maxine, is a social worker who finds safe havens for abused children. Maxine is played by Tyne Daly in her no-nonsense, take-no-prisoners persona. She is a woman of principle and passion, so committed to her work that she is reluctant to marry a handsome billionaire who wants her to travel with him to the exotic locations to which his business takes him.

In an episode so memorable I can communicate the gist of it from memory, Maxine explodes in anger on two occasions, one of which involves a woman who is an important political ally to her agency. This threatens her boss because the buck stops with him, and he reprimands Maxine. He tells her that to keep her job she has to take an anger management class. She reluctantly attends, only to be greeted by a mind-numbing instructor who is a caricature of the worst of personal growth nightmares. He is so ingratiating you want to puke listening to him.

First the instructor leads the group in a guided exercise, asking them to imagine themselves in a place of ease and relaxation; Maxine visualizes herself sitting astride a white horse on a beautiful merry-go-round on a warm summer's day. The instructor then asks the class to imagine their anger as a red ball that becomes smaller and smaller and therefore manageable. In her imagination, however, Maxine's red ball becomes a sphere of fire that gets bigger and more frightening as she ducks lower each time it whizzes by her.

After the visualization, the instructor places a red marble into the hands of a person in the class with directions to "express your anger into this marble and then pass it on." One by one as the marble is passed, people speak of their frustration with such things as traffic snarls, gaining five pounds from eating a one-pound box of chocolates, telemarketers calling at dinnertime, and other perceived travesties. When Maxine receives the marble, she cannot restrain herself. "What makes me angry," she ventures, "is a father who puts out his cigarette on his baby's skin. A mother who throws a newborn into a dumpster." As she gains momentum, reciting even more graphic descriptions of the tragedies she sees every day, the other participants react with predictable shock.

After a passionate display of the horrors of child abuse, she passes on the marble only to grab it back a second later and exclaim, "But what really pisses me off is a room full of supposed adults who think that *traffic* . . . and *telemarketers* . . . and *fat thighs* . . . are worth getting *angry* about!"

With that, she stands and leaves with a flourish, turning at the doorway to pocket the marble and say, "Thanks! I think I feel better now."

I discussed this rousing scene with Dr. Margaret Paul, psychologist and author of *Inner Bonding*, who said what Maxine expressed was not anger. Anger can be used to remain stuck in being a victim, as demonstrated by the insipid responses of the others in the anger management group. Instead, Margaret explained, Maxine spoke her outrage, which is the response of a true loving adult to injustice. Outrage comes from our essence and motivates us to take loving action, while anger is an ego response that keeps us stuck in blame and powerlessness.

So speak out whenever you are given the opportunity. The power of a story—or a thousand and one stories if that's what it takes—can change the future of the kingdom.

Remember Scheherazade? Her father was a trusted advisor to the Persian king Shahryār, a benevolent ruler until he learned his wife had betrayed him. Rather than risk the pain and humiliation of a woman's infidelity a second time, he ordered Scheherazade's father to bring a virgin to his bedchambers each night and put her to death the following morning, the same fate that befell his wife.

When the sadness and loss grew unbearable and the future of the kingdom was in peril, Scheherazade approached her father and asked to go to the king that night. Not wanting to send his daughter to a certain death, he resisted mightily. But she begged until he relented.

When she stood before the king, she asked whether she might say good-night to her sister. He agreed, and when her sister arrived, she asked Scheherazade to tell her just one final story, which she did as the king listened. Before finishing her tale, she feigned drowsiness and drifted off to sleep. The king was so captivated by her story that he delayed her execution and asked her to continue her story a second night, then a third, a fourth, a fifth . . . until after 1,001 nights he grew to love her and trust her. Scheherazade became his queen and the kingdom was saved.

Although it is good to define our perfect audience, God sometimes says, "Ha!" Scheherazade surely would have preferred to tell her stories to a friendly audience at a festival rather than to a tyrant. Yet she chose to step forward to offer her gift of storytelling and in so doing saved countless lives and returned the king to his true nature.

Likewise, your preparation to speak compellingly equips you for assignments you may not foresee even though you have an ideal audience in mind. In my own case, I decided to focus my business on working with people who, recalling Gandhi's famous quotation, are the change they want to see in the world. It then occurred to me that fully realized humans neither need training nor represent a very large market! I revised my target clientele as "people who are *becoming* the change they want to see in the world."

As individuals and as a planet, we are on a hero's journey with much to learn. The challenges ahead will increase our collective capacity and wisdom to *be* the change. Our individual call to excellence is to express our original medicine and stay awake to our lives and the world around us as we grow in our power to live a better story. In the meantime, let's tell stories that call forth our collective imagination and greatness.

12

Tell a Better Story

Inspiring the Impossible

There is a wonderful excerpt from *Alice in Wonderland* that suggests we can dream impossible things into being. When Alice declares to the Queen of Hearts, "One can't believe impossible things!" the Queen responds: "I daresay you haven't had much practice. When I was your age, I always did it for half an hour a day. Why, sometimes I've believed as many as six impossible things before breakfast."

Although it is easy to accept old stories as truth, take a lesson from the Navajo, masters of weaving. If you look closely at their exquisite rugs, you'll notice there is always an imperfection. This "defect" is by design, creating a place where the Great Spirit can continue to enter. Likewise, any story we tell ourselves is unfinished. We're still here, part of the web of life, and we care about making a difference. Spirit has an opening through which to work.

There are many weavers of better stories today whose life paths have led them to the right opening to accomplish something that moves others into the realm of the previously impossible. Although Al Gore may have thought his greatest contribution would be as president of the United States, the Great Mystery clearly had other plans. When he was relieved of the political burden of balancing all causes, he returned to the one that had his name on it: climate

change. In the process, he lightened up and became an impas-
sioned speaker, arousing the world from its deep slumber on the
issue and winning an Emmy, an Oscar, and the 2007 Nobel Peace
Prize. His earlier wooden style never struck me as the real Al Gore
anyway, because we'd witnessed his humanity when he left the Sen-
ate to rush to the side of his young son, critically injured when he
was hit by a car.

When Gore was in the presidential race, a Tennessee colleague
told me he had coached him for the debates. I mentioned that I'd
sure like to work with him. "What would you do?" he asked.

"I'd get him alone in a room with no political advisors in sight
and find out what he loves," I replied. "I'd suggest he make it his
platform and speak from his heart."

My colleague laughed. "You're so naive."

Impossible Dreamers

Carol Newell inherited a family fortune in her thirties, when she
already knew what she valued and was engaged in causes that
called to her. After putting aside the funds to maintain a modest
lifestyle, she partnered with a trusted friend, social entrepreneur
Joel Solomon, to activate her wealth in support of a sustainable
economy in British Columbia. She remained behind the scenes for
ten years. When she stepped to the forefront prepared to put her
mouth where her money is, it was to Play BIG, the name she gave
her plan to empower people of wealth to revolutionize the money
rules they live by to create transformational change. Now anyone
with $15 million or more and a heart for change has access to a
working model for harnessing personal wealth to fuel sustainability and social justice. In 2006, Carol was inducted into the Order
of Canada in recognition of her capacity to play big.

Although it is unlikely you will be knighted or awarded a Nobel
Peace Prize, your commitment to a noble cause is the foundation
of a better story. Join me in the front row for another.

In 2007, Andrew Harvey took the stage in a packed ballroom in Santa Fe to talk about "sacred activism." His poetic expression, sophisticated humor, and Oxford accent were mesmerizing but did little to ease the vivid enumeration of the relentless horror, insanity, and great death of our times. After several minutes he paused and said, "And if that were all I had to say to you, I would have prepared a large vat of Jim Jones Kool-Aid and we would all join hands and sing 'Kumbaya.'"

After the collective sigh of relief, Andrew continued his passionate appeal, asking that we understand in the deepest possible way that the immense chaos we are experiencing is not the sign of a final destruction. Instead, it is the Great Mother inviting us, with fierce compassion, to face our heartbreak, not try to escape it. Only if we allow our hearts to be slashed open will we drop the veil of separation and, in Andrew's words, "surrender to the massive transformation that invites us forward to engage in the monumental birth process of a new kind of humanity that is already taking place on this earth."

As examples of the respect for life so dear to the Mother's heart, Andrew spoke of Nelson Mandela, Desmond Tutu, and F. W. de Klerk working together to end apartheid in South Africa; the Dalai Lama's extraordinary witness to compassion in the face of genocide; Gandhi's refusal to use violence to unseat the British Empire; and Martin Luther King Jr.'s embodiment of forgiveness. Avoiding false promises that change will occur without disruption and pain, he beseeched the audience to develop the spiritual practices that will keep our hearts open. Hearing the new story he told, one that urges each of us to renew our relationships with ourselves, each other, and all of creation, we knew his message came from the core of his being, rousing us from our stupor to face a crisis so immense it is galvanizing humanity to undertake a new beginning for the entire human race. Together through the energies of love and sacred activism, Andrew tells us, "our children, godchildren, and grandchildren can inherit an immeasurably more beautiful and just world."

One of the most honest, inspiring, and transformative speeches I have ever witnessed, Andrew's presentation contained it all: heart and head, passion and humor, politics and religion, sex and drugs. We left the room inspired to rock and roll. Months later there was still a buzz about the better story he told about our capacity to shape our future. Without trying to provide answers to what is unknowable, he illuminated a path for others, much like the one described by Janice Becker Haynes in her poem, "Illumination," written to commemorate the 2007 Real Speaking graduate reunion:

You who hold tenderly the journey
the breath of life
breathe
You who hold passion and joy
the fire of life
burn
You who hold hands with a little child
learn to follow that child
explore
You who wander with no purpose
enjoy firefly moments
hike to clear waterfalls
until your inner knowing
forms a path for your feet
You who teach, wise ones,
so full of life
having lived well
willing to guide
remember to continue on your own journey
You may turn your back to others
We see the light you follow
blazing around you
and go to seek our own.

Telling a better story and knowing people will be inspired to find a way to contribute that reflects their own original medicine requires faith, hope, and trust:

Faith that we are exactly where we need to be, with a front-row
seat for the most transformative times imaginable.

Hope that the changes afoot will call us forward collectively to
create the world we envision.

Trust that when we reveal who we are by speaking what matters
most we will align with our soul families and together create
a new reality.

Change agents want a world that works for everyone—that's the
genuine hope of most people, even when we don't see how to get
from here to there. This is not to suggest that we will be ushered
into a new story without disruption.

We are living on the edge of chaos. We can't control weather
patterns, earth shifts, or other people. At the same time, as José
Stevens, psychotherapist and author of *The Power Path*, reminds us,
"This edge holds the most creative energy, the highest potential and
the greatest possibilities." While we'd like to think we can transcend
the upheaval of our times, José reminds us of the chaos of renovat-
ing a home, pointing out that when we hold a vision of what we want,
we then can weather the disruption, knowing it leads to something
far better. But we have to knock down the walls and begin.

In her best-selling book *The Year of Magical Thinking*, Joan Didion
wrote of the sudden death of her husband and the ensuing year
of expecting he would show up at any moment to confirm it was
all a terrible mistake. Using that same type of magical thinking,
many of us shield ourselves from the trauma of our times, believing someone else will know how to navigate the turbulence and
lead us to safer shores. The Hopi prophecy "We are the ones we
have been waiting for" moves us from self-insulation and denial to
action.

We can begin in the places we are shattered: "Break my heart,
oh break it again, so I can love even more again," Rumi says. Hearing that, your first response, like mine, might be, "Is he nuts?"
Yet there is deep wisdom in being willing to experience our greatest anguish as a barometer of our greatest gift. As David Whyte's
poem "The Well of Grief," offered in chapter 3, reminds us, our

descent into the depths of sorrow allows us to retrieve "those small round coins thrown by those who wished for something else." Those coins represent the glimmer of a better story as we recover the voice lost when we first refused to slip into the place where our hearts would break open. In reclaiming that voice, we discover what is ours to do and we begin to act, recognizing that although we can't do everything, we can do something. Tzeporah Berman, cofounder of Forest Ethics, reminds us, "We are responsible in this era not only for what we do but also for what we do not do."

José Stevens notes that, as old structures are swept away, the void left behind leaves an "I-don't-know" place we avoid because we think we will not survive it. "There are times there is little information at the surface level but a great deal gestating below the surface," he says, "similar to a garden that has been seeded where only small blades of green are apparent. There is a grand tide of novel ideas, good solutions, and better ways of living already making its way into our consciousness. But first we have to make room for it." Following are ten better stories representing the grand tide of which José speaks, making a difference in the empowerment of youth and women, human rights, health, finance, education, environment, business, and communications. Each initiative is as personal and original as the medicine of the person who was inspired to act.

Van Jones, who heads the Ella Baker Center for Human Rights in Oakland, California, helps his audiences to get real about thinking that poor people who may not make it out of their neighborhoods alive will sign on to saving the polar bears. His passion is to build a pathway out of poverty with green-collar jobs that include retrofitting buildings across America with solar panels, building wind farms, and delivering new sources of "work, wealth, and health while honoring the earth." An acclaimed speaker, he reminds his audience that "Martin Luther King, Jr. didn't change the world by announcing, 'I have a complaint!'" Van works with what is and is committed to a dream of moving disaffected youth to the ground floor of the burgeoning solar industry.

Barbara Dossey, PhD, RN, a trailblazer in holistic nursing, has devoted her career to setting standards of excellence in health care. Author of *Florence Nightingale: Mystic, Visionary, Healer,* Barbara applies the inspiring story of a woman who was a spiritual beacon for all who suffer to inform and empower nurses worldwide to become "21st-century Nightingales." She cofounded the Nightingale Institute for Global Health (NIGH) to build a grassroots movement among nurses globally to adopt health as the universal priority and to band together to actively share what works to create a healthy world.

While working for a hospital in 1991, Cliff Feigenbaum decided to investigate where his employer invested his 401K funds. He was shocked to discover that his retirement plan included large holdings of tobacco stocks. Building on his own interest in aligning his money with his values, he started a newsletter that advised others to do the same, from the way they shop to the way they invest. Early on, most people wondered what he was talking about, but Cliff persevered, believing that *GreenMoney Journal* was his to do in the world. In 2007, to much fanfare, Cliff celebrated the journal's fifteenth year of publication. The world had finally caught up with a better story: namely, you can both make money and make a difference.

Tom Brady, whose graduate studies in philosophy inform his perceptive astrology readings, would tell us that the architecture of the solar system at the time of one's birth is an image of the person one has the potential to become. As this image realizes itself over time, it becomes a story or "life myth"—the word *myth* having originally meant "one's truest or deepest story." Part of Tom's story was thinking of himself as a loner who didn't get involved in causes. However, seeing the threat to his own place of refuge as the beloved national forests near his Santa Fe home were invaded by ATVs changed all that. He engaged in local activism, saying, "This is my destiny." He has chosen to use his voice through writing articles.

Priya Haji founded World of Good, a company that in just three years distributed fair-trade handcrafts from more than five thousand artisans in thirty-four countries to more than a thousand retail partners. Those artisans, responsible for an estimated 22,700 dependents, are able to feed their families while sharing the beauty of their cultures. Hearing Priya speak and watching her take the stage is witnessing mastery. Dressed in a gorgeous turquoise sari, reminding us of the women of the world she represents, she shares her story and her struggles with humility and profound appreciation.

Charles Kouns founded Imagine Learning, an organization seeking to build a new educational experience for teenagers based upon one question: "How do we educate young people to thrive in a world of possibility?" Charles believes that the current educational structure was created around 1850 based upon the question "How do we educate young people to be productive citizens and workers in an industrial society?" Now in the process of asking young people in nearly fifty countries around the world to cocreate a vision of the learning experience in which they would love to participate, he holds listening sessions to hear their answers. These "listenings" conclude with each group creating their vision in a large painting. His dream is to assemble these paintings into one, thus giving a collective voice to teenagers around the world. Ultimately, he intends to introduce a new educational concept that will answer Imagine Learning's question anywhere in the world so that young people *will* thrive in a world of possibility.

Kim Reynolds of Mind Over Mountains, a coaching firm that empowers women through outdoor adventures, grew to love the people of Nepal. As an expedition leader to the unclimbed West Ridge of Pumori in the Himalaya, she raised money for The Friendship House, a haven for seventeen Nepali girls at risk of child labor, abuse, being raised in jail by their parents, or being sold into the sex trade. Kim kept the house open by raising nearly $30,000. For the first time, reaching the Pumori summit seemed insignificant compared to the smiles, the hugs, and the gratitude that came from the girls' hearts. That expedition changed Kim. From then on, her outdoor pursuits included giving back with the intention of inspiring the outdoor community to do the same. She cofounded the dZi Foundation and Chicks with Picks, an organization that offers ice climbing clinics for women. Chicks with Picks has raised $136,000 for women's shelters in Colorado. It's business as usual for Kim, who asks one simple question: "If we don't take care of each other on this planet, who will?"

Victoria Castle, author of *The Trance of Scarcity*, and a group of colleagues started looking at where the planet was headed and decided they were unwilling to sit back and wish it wasn't so. Recognizing that "as women get older we get bolder," they developed Hot Women for a Cool Planet to help women consume consciously, influence boldly, and contribute purposefully. You can take The Hot Women Pledge at www.hotwomenforacoolplanet.com, and it is not a vow to be taken lightly. It asks you to commit to specific actions to leverage the power of uniting our voices and actions. According to the website, when signing the pledge, you agree to:

- Find every opportunity to connect with others and initiate conversations about our shared future and what we can do together in our neighborhoods, workplaces, schools, etc.
- Begin each day by using your power of creativity to visualize a healthy world at peace and send love to all beings, knowing that this "invisible" act changes the world.
- Find a way to support at least one woman less fortunate than yourself and practice gratitude for the life you have.
- Take accountability for your own well-being—physically, mentally, emotionally, and spiritually—so that you are a resilient, renewable resource. You will keep a light heart, an open mind, and a generous spirit.

Russell Precious describes himself as an "ecopreneur." With several successful business ventures to his credit, the most recent Pharmaca Integrative Pharmacies, he sees himself not as a businessman but rather as a man who does business as a culture-changing activity. His studies in history provide the perspective to remind us that since the end of World War II the boomer generation in North America has lived largely in a perfect "nonstorm," with relative peace and stability and an abundance of goods and services. Although those factors have allowed us to tackle some of the societal issues that needed to be addressed, such as civil rights, women's issues, the environment, and more, he notes that we can't ignore the fact that dark times are nothing new. In fact, what modern culture considers normal in the context of ten thousand years is a blip. Whether he is quoting Rumi—"Ours is not a caravan of despair"—or Dylan—"He not busy being born is busy dying"—he inspires hope, collaboration, and connection, suggesting that the issues before us are so big that the pettiness of differences has got to go.

Paul Jay, CEO of the Real News Network, says, "When covering world news, we understand there are two worlds, one that is dying and the other coming into being. People can't just fight against the old; they also have to advocate for the new. The Real News Network has emerged to focus on stories that face facts about the world as it is and inspire people to see the world as it could be. Believing that "the future depends on knowing," the Real News Network (www.therealnews.com) does not accept advertising or government and corporate funding and instead relies on individual viewers for its financial support. This ensures its independence in choosing the news and stories it covers.

There are better stories everywhere you look. Paul Hawken estimates that there are well over a million organizations across the globe working toward ecological sustainability and social justice. His book *Blessed Unrest* is full of examples of what is going right in the world. Hold in your heart the folks who work for positive change in every arena, even if you don't personally relate to the issue. Each person who takes a stand based on what he or she loves is doing his or her part to mend the web of life, even though none of us knows what our future holds. In choosing where to serve, the most important voice to listen to is your own.

Carolyn Forché said to me of her 2006 cancer diagnosis, "People hear of my illness and tell me I'll be okay. They don't know that. I know they mean well, but they are saying what *they* want to believe, to make themselves feel better. No one knows—I certainly don't—and to pretend they do is a way of avoiding the stark reality of what I live with every day. The greatest gift another person can give me is their willingness to be in the uncertainty with me."

Just as a critical diagnosis brings immediacy to deciding what matters most on a personal level, our uncertain global future also commands discernment. Crafting a new reality disturbs our old ways of being; living with and through chaos, with all its cues to remind us that we are not in control, conspires to make us real, which is another way of saying knowing and expressing our truth, full of humanity and accessible to others. *The Velveteen Rabbit*, by Margery Williams, promises, "Once you are Real, you can't become unreal again. It lasts for always."

"What is REAL?" asked the Rabbit one day. "Does it mean having things that buzz inside you and a stick out handle?"

"Real isn't how you are made," said the Skin Horse. "It's a thing that happens to you. When a child loves you for a long, long time, not just to play with, but REALLY loves you, then you become Real."

"Does it hurt?" asked the Rabbit.

"Sometimes," said the Skin Horse, for he was always truthful. "When you are Real, you don't mind being hurt."

"Does it happen all at once, like being wound up," he asked, "or bit by bit?"

"It doesn't happen all at once," said the Skin Horse. "You become. It takes a long time. That's why it doesn't happen to people who break easily, or have sharp edges, or who have to be carefully kept. Generally, by the time you are Real, most of your hair has been loved off, and your eyes drop out and you get loose in the joints and very shabby. But these things don't matter at all, because once you are Real, you can't be ugly, except to people who don't understand."

I often tell this story when people ask, "Am I too old to be a speaker? At my age, who wants to listen?" For starters, I ask them how much they would trust someone decades younger to provide the guidance they seek for themselves. Then I enjoy watching their dawning realization that they are, in fact, in just the right place at the right time. Having witnessed the wisdom they hold, it saddens me that our culture is so intoxicated by youth that we often discount the gift of the elders. Respecting the contributions and interfacing with all generations is critical to understanding the whole so that new solutions can be created.

Angeles Arrien is changing the story on aging with her book and workshops on *The Second Half of Life*. She notes, "When you find the courage to change at mid life, a miracle happens. Your character is opened, deepened, strengthened, softened. You return to your soul's highest values. You are now prepared to create your legacy: an imprint of your dream for our world."

When asked by an audience member at Whidbey Institute the most important practice in navigating these challenging times, eco-philosopher and Buddhist scholar Joanna Macy responded, "Gratitude. Gratitude for being alive right now to be part of this adventure. When you embark on an adventure, you don't know how it will turn out. In a glad adventure, it doesn't matter how it turns out because you are fully engaged."

In *Legend of the Rainbow Warriors*, Steven McFadden reveals a prophecy handed down through generations of Native Americans that heralds a new story for today. It foretells a time when people young and old, of all colors and all faiths, recognize that the way we live is destructive to ourselves and to Mother Earth. These wise "rainbow warriors" embody healthy, respectful ways of living and set in motion a joyous era of regeneration and peace where the earth once again flourishes.

Will this hopeful myth penetrate world culture sufficiently to make a positive difference? Rather than waiting for the historians to answer this question, may you fully engage in this glad adventure with your original medicine and true voice to express the fullness of the gifts and wisdom you hold. May you discover the better story your life has prepared you to tell. And may you ask your ancestors for assistance, remembering that we each have a circle of support that joins us the moment we are conceived and is with us until we leave our bodies. They stand behind us and ask, "Will this be the one? Will this be the one—the one who will break the harmful patterns for this generation and the generations to come?"

May we be the ones.

Resources

Written Communications to Support a Professional Presentation

Throughout the speaking process, your written communications are vital reinforcement to the outcome you want to achieve. Handling them with skill is a hallmark of a pro. These communications include the program description, fee schedule, letter of agreement, room setup request, prearrival questions, informational handouts, evaluation form, and other documents. Definitions and examples of each follow.

Program Description

Whether you are seeking speaking engagements or responding to inquiries, clients want a program description that will "speak to" their group. When it's time to describe your carefully crafted speech or workshop, writing a program description that stands out—and attracts the people who will benefit from your wisdom— is an essential marketing skill for speakers.

To draw people to programs at Hollyhock Retreat Centre on Cortes Island in British Columbia, presenters are asked to respond to "clarifying questions." Once answered, a professional copywriter develops a program description for the catalog. Hollyhock asked me to describe my Spirited Speaking program—including bio—in no more than 175 words. It seemed like a tough assignment, but their clarifying questions were invaluable in focusing my thinking.

Their process allows you to write first for yourself, a principle recommended by communications specialist Isabel Parlett of Parlance Communications. It is similar to exploring your own home zone material for your speaking—important to discovery but not yet ready for publication. The six questions Hollyhock asks are ones to consider when you are writing your own copy. They are listed below, along with my responses to provide a sample of what they created from the information I provided.

1. What makes your program unique/compelling?

Public speaking is usually taught as a series of techniques that cause people to be removed from their true passion and to distrust their originality. At Spirited Speaking, they get to revel in their magnificence as who they really are comes to the forefront through group processes, dyads, and fun!

2. What would you most like conveyed about your workshop?

That there is nothing to fear about authentic self-expression. In fact, it is where we experience our greatest power and where we learn to appreciate and trust ourselves.

3. What will participants learn?

- How to access their home zone, the place of their personal power and authentic expression
- How to make an emotional connection with others through stories
- How to diffuse hostility
- How to have a courageous conversation
- How to speak with confidence and clarity in both introductions and professional presentations

4. How are participants going to learn? What exercises will they be doing?

- Exploring deeper issues in dyads
- Speaking out to the full group about their discoveries
- Practicing speaking from the home zone
- Receiving coaching in the four primary speaking skills
- Learning inner tools to support outer success

5. What are the benefits of taking this workshop?

Participants will enjoy increased capacity to speak in public with confidence and success, a deeper connection to self and the message that is their unique gift to the world, and excitement about being heard.

6. For whom is the program designed?

This program is for anyone who wants to improve his or her capacity to speak out and be heard. The skills are applicable no matter the participant's age or profession; however, it is important that they want to draw on their inner life and experience and be real rather than get "fixed." It's great for mature teens —this is the time to learn this!

These questions focused my thinking to draft my program description on page 169, which they edited, for Spirited Speaking.

SAMPLE PROGRAM DESCRIPTION

Spirited Speaking

Bring your speaking alive. Expand your capacity to speak out and be heard. The ability to move others has little to do with your facts and information. It comes from eliminating fear and distrust of expressing your deepest values. In this lively experiential program, give voice to what has fire and meaning for you and explore speaking from your home zone, your place of personal power and authenticity. Bring your speaking alive and get results by making an emotional connection with others so they hear what you are saying.

Spirited Speaking is an experience that takes you to the heart of what you want to say. Rather than imposing technique that removes you from your passion, the class will guide you to learn to trust your inherent capacity to communicate, celebrating your individuality and originality. Then we'll move to the heart of speaking, where you'll receive personal tips to demonstrate how small changes make a big difference in your capacity to reach an audience.

We emerge with a clear statement of our gifts and talents, of what's real in our lives, and what's next. These final statements are videotaped to take home.

Gail Larsen is the founder of Real Speaking, the premier presentations program for people of purpose and catalysts of change. She is an award-winning entrepreneur (U.S. Small Business Administration) and formerly served as executive vice president of the worldwide National Speakers Association. She is the author of *Transformational Speaking: If You Want to Change the World, Tell a Better Story.* On a lighter note, she is also the author of *Madame Ovary: Midlife as an Art Form.* www.realspeaking.net

Fee Schedule

A professional speaker has established fees, which vary according to type and length of the presentation or workshop. Speaking fees have less to do with the time spent presenting than with the importance of the session to the overall conference. For example, a one-hour keynote will command a much higher fee than a breakout or preconference training session. The competition for keynote slots is intense and usually is a one-time engagement no matter how well received because at the next conference a new headliner

SAMPLE FEE SCHEDULE

Engaging Madame Ovary as Your Speaker

Madame Ovary is available to speak for a variety of occasions, from dynamic keynotes to festive high teas. Each program is designed to address the needs of your group and is delivered with humor, wisdom, and—of course—*style*!

Speaking Fees

KEYNOTES AND PRESENTATIONS UP TO ONE HOUR:

$ amount + travel expenses

$ amount [typically lower] for local engagements with
no overnight travel

HALF-DAY WORKSHOPS

$ amount + travel expenses

$ amount for local engagements with no overnight travel

FULL-DAY WORKSHOPS

$ amount + travel expenses

$ amount for local engagements with no overnight travel

Madame Ovary is happy to speak to two groups on the same day (for example, a keynote presentation and breakout session or workshop) as long as there are reasonable breaks between sessions.

[Note if there is any state tax to be paid on professional fees.]
Speaking fees are commissionable to speakers bureaus at _____ (typically 25%).

Reserving a Date with Madame Ovary

Your date with Madame Ovary is reserved with a nonrefundable deposit of 50% of the speaking fee, with the balance due within 14 days of the completed engagement. A Letter of Agreement will be sent to confirm all arrangements.

Travel from Whidbey Island, Washington

Expenses are billed following the engagement and are payable within 14 days. They include:

Round-trip airline service from Seattle (coach class in U.S./Canada)
Inspiring overnight accommodations (nonsmoking)
Yummy meals, including chocolate
Ground transportation, parking, and lavish tips

"Amazing grace how sweet the sound of Madame Ovary, addressing her followers with nuggets of wisdom-drenched comedy." *—Santa Fe Reporter*

is needed to promote attendance. On the other hand, successful workshop leaders are invited to return.

A sample fee schedule for Madame Ovary is included on page 171 and reflects some of the possible variables to consider, such as whether you will charge less when you don't have to travel out of town or overnight. Setting fees is an individual matter; if speaking is not your primary source of income, often receiving a fee is not a consideration. When it is, I recommend you charge so that you can show up with a happy heart. When you make an exception to your stated fee, always ask for something in exchange, such as a second airline ticket and/or extra nights of accommodations if you wish to extend your stay, a mailing list for the group, on-site support to sell your books after the presentation, a free conference registration, an ad in the conference program, or something else of value to you.

Letter of Agreement

All arrangements agreed upon verbally are best confirmed in writing. This letter, to be signed and returned to you to verify the details you have listed, assures that you and your client are operating from the same understanding. Memories are short, and a confirmation while the conversation is fresh saves much consternation and misunderstanding later on.

I previously used letters of agreement only for programs where I was receiving a professional fee. No longer. After agreeing verbally to present a keynote for a group for less than my standard fee at the request of a friend, I was asked whether I would be willing to also be the emcee for the half-day program following my talk. In the joy of cocreation, I agreed. When I received the early promotion, I was listed as the emcee with no mention of my keynote! It was challenging and awkward to move back to keynote from footnote.

Some speakers and speakers bureaus have extensive contracts with much fine print; however, keeping it simple has worked consistently over time for me. Below is a list of the information I include in a letter of agreement:

Client Contact Information

- Organization
- Mailing address
- Physical address
- Name of event
- Representative's name and title
- Representative's phone numbers (office, cell, and home)
- Emergency contact and phone
- Fax
- Email

Details of the Presentation(s)

- Date
- Time
- Title
- Name of venue
- Location of venue
- Phone number of venue
- Name of on-site contact
- On-site contact's phone (office, cell, and home)
- Audience (estimated number and demographics)
- Equipment requested
- Room setup requested
- If you will be selling or signing books, note time and place. If you need sales support, ask in advance. If the hosting organization is ordering books, include instructions and contact info for placing the order.

Fee and Expenses

- Fee
- Terms of payment (It is customary to ask for 50 percent with the signed agreement to reserve the date, with the remainder to billed with expenses to be reimbursed to be paid within 30 days of the program.)

- Add a note that the date requested will be held until 10 to 14 days after the time of your verbal agreement and is confirmed with receipt of your deposit.
- Ask for a signed copy of the agreement to be returned with your deposit and provide the name in which payment should be issued and the mailing address.
- Travel expenses. Include whatever you have agreed upon (airfare, car rental, mileage, accommodations, meals, parking, etc., or per diem).
- Cancellation policy. Decide what works for you if it is necessary for your client to cancel. Typically, the deposit is not refundable because you have held the date and declined other opportunities. If an emergency situation should cause you to cancel, consider whether you would be able to provide a replacement.

Acceptance and Signatures

- Provide space for signatures—yours and your client's.
- Include a line for the client to add his or her title as an authorized representative of the organization.

Other Communications

If you are speaking to a group with a planner assigned to the event, you will receive a list of what they need from you with a timetable. Otherwise, keeping communications on track becomes your responsibility. Once the engagement is confirmed, mark your calendar to send the following to your client:

1. Program description, as covered earlier, to be sent with room setup and equipment requests (placement of lectern, type of microphone, flip chart and markers, audio/visual, etc.).
2. Prearrival questions, such as significant challenges the group faces, program schedule and names of other speakers, key people whose names you should know, name of your introducer, who will meet your flight, suggested attire, etc. See pages 175–176 for an example of a prearrival questionnaire.

SAMPLE PREARRIVAL QUESTIONNAIRE

[Speaker's Name]
Meeting Questionnaire for [Organization/Company Name]
Date of Meeting _____
Time of Meeting _____   a.m. ____   p.m. ____

Thank you for taking time to fill out this questionnaire. In order for [SPEAKER]
to contribute all he possibly can to the theme and purpose of your meeting, please
respond to the following questions. The few minutes required will be more than
compensated by the increased effectiveness of his presentation. Your success and
the success of your meeting are his mission. (Skip any questions that do not apply.)

Address __ _____ _____
_____

Phone(s) (___) _____   (___)_____
Fax (___)_____
Email _____   Website _____

Meeting Site (City, State) _____ __
Hotel Accommodations (Name) _____ _____
Address _____
_____

Phone (___) _____
Fax (___)_____

Name of this particular group: _____
Commonly used nickname and/or acronym/initials: ___ _____
Commonly used advertising slogan or organization's motto:
_____

Primary contact person(s) at the meeting site: _____
Cell phone: (___) _____

Names of the top senior personnel (and spouse, if in attendance) at
meeting (CEO, chairman of the board, president, vice presidents, board
members, etc.): _____
_____
_____
_____
_____

[SPEAKER] will be introduced by _____
Title _____

(continued)

SAMPLE PREARRIVAL QUESTIONNAIRE *(continued)*

Audience size _____ _____ % male _____ % female

Age Ranges: 20–30 yrs. ___%   30–40 ___%   40–50 ___ %   50+ ___%

Audience Makeup (i.e., top executives, managers and spouses, clients, etc.)
_____

U.S. Audience ____%   International Audience Members ____%

Dress code for principals _____

Appropriate speaker attire _____

Theme and purpose of meeting:
_____
_____

What takes place immediately before SPEAKER'S presentation?
_____
_____

After his presentation?
_____
_____

Current or immediate past successes of organization:
_____
_____

Current or immediate past challenges within your organization or industry:
_____
_____
_____
_____

Foreseeable future difficulties or challenges:
_____
_____
_____

Bottom line, what do you hope for SPEAKER to accomplish with his presentation?
_____
_____
_____

Please complete this questionnaire and fax or email it with any related program material no later than 3 weeks prior to the engagement.

If you feel a conference call would be helpful, please call to arrange it.

Thank you!

Please return to: [email address or fax number]

3. Introduction, written by you, as described in chapter 8. Send
   it to the introducer in advance—and take an extra copy with
   you. Remember to read it aloud before you send it to make
   sure it sounds the way you talk. Short sentences are conversational; long ones are hard to follow. Include only the essential
   elements of your background that indicate your credibility
   to be addressing your topic. People can likely read about you
   in the program, and you want your introducer to pique their
   interest, not put them to sleep with a recitation of your entire
   professional history. The last line should lead in to the beginning of your presentation. Include a request to the introducer
   not to deviate from what you've written.

4. Travel arrangements, notifying your client once they are in
   place. Confirm how you will make your way to the program
   venue. If someone is to meet you, be specific about time and
   location and exchange cell phone numbers. Confirm your on-
   site contact and how to reach that person in an emergency.

On-Site Communications

Handouts. Providing a handout with useful information, including
your contact information, helps you develop a relationship with
your audience while reinforcing your message. Typically, the organizers will photocopy the handout for you if you send it at least a
few weeks ahead. Determine in advance how you want it distributed. If there are sessions opposite yours, people sometimes drop
by for the handout and move on. Other times they read far ahead
of you and don't attune to the presentation. For that reason, consider providing handouts at the close of the session or by email to
those who leave their cards to request it. (This practice also builds
your mailing list.) As an audience member, I sometimes find it
annoying not to have the handout to make notes as I listen. As
a speaker, I find it more disconcerting if people are reading my
handout instead of listening to me! Another strategy is to include

a bonus handout that contains information not included in your talk so it is a clear add-on rather than reinforcement.

Evaluations. If the event organizers do not plan to ask for an evaluation of your session, consider asking for your own to garner feedback and potentially useful testimonials. Be sure to let your client know you plan to distribute an evaluation and include time for it to be completed at the end of your session. It is rare to receive specific feedback if you don't ask for it in the moment. A small gift or special handout to those who return it to you on site is a helpful incentive.

Questions to ask in an evaluation include:

1. Rate the value of the presentation (using a scale of 1–5 or 1–10).
2. What was most useful to you?
3. What would you have liked more of? Less of?
4. What would you say to someone else about this program?

Question 4 garners useful testimonial material, so if you're looking for quotes ask for the person's name and permission to use what he or she said.

Follow-up Communications

A thank-you note to your host is always in order. Include your invoice for any fees due and travel costs that are to be reimbursed. Ask for the evaluations, feedback received, or suggestions. If you have a colleague or suggestions for speakers for future events, offer your recommendation. Referrals from a trusted source are the primary way speakers are hired.

May each speaking engagement you complete be an opportunity to change the world by telling a better story!

Bibliography

Arrien, Angeles. *The Four-Fold Way: Walking the Paths of the Warrior, Teacher, Healer, and Visionary.* San Francisco: HarperSanFrancisco, 1993.

———. *The Second Half of Life: Opening the Eight Gates of Wisdom.* Louisville, CO: Sounds True, 2005.

Brown, Juanita, and David Isaacs. *The World Café: Shaping Our Futures Through Conversations That Matter.* San Francisco: Berrett-Koehler Publishers, 2005.

Fritz, Robert. *The Path of Least Resistance: Learning to Become the Creative Force in Your Own Life.* New York: Ballantine Books, 1984.

Gladwell, Malcolm. *The Tipping Point: How Little Things Can Make a Big Difference.* New York: Little Brown and Company, 2002.

Hawken, Paul. *Blessed Unrest: How the Largest Movement in the World Came into Being and Why No One Saw It Coming.* New York: Viking, 2007.

Hawkins, *David R. Power vs. Force: The Hidden Determinants of Human Behavior.* Carlsbad, CA: Hay House, 1995.

I Ching or Book of Changes. 3rd ed. Translated by Richard Wilhelm and Cary F. Baynes. Princeton: Princeton University Press, 1967.

Ingerman, Sandra. *How to Heal Toxic Thoughts: Simple Tools for Personal Transformation.* New York: Sterling Publishing, 2007.

Institute of Cultural Affairs. *Group Facilitation Methods.* Chicago: The Institute of Cultural Affairs, 1991.

La Sha, Kelly. *Liquid Mirror.* Albuquerque, NM: Landings, 2008.

McFadden, Steven. *Legend of the Rainbow Warriors.* Lincoln, NE: iUniverse, 1995.

Meilleur, Roberta. *World Dance: A Joyful Path to Free Movement and Personal Growth.* Courtenay, BC: Free & Footloose Publications, 2001. Available at www.RobertaMeilleur.com.

Nattrass, Brian, and Mary Altomare. *Dancing with the Tiger: Learning Sustainability Step by Natural Step.* Gabriola Island, BC: New Society Publishers, 2002.

Omega Institute for Holistic Studies. *Omega Talk, Summer 2002.* Rhinebeck, New York: Omega Institute for Holistic Studies, 2002.

Orloff, Judith. *Positive Energy: 10 Extraordinary Prescriptions for Transforming Fatigue, Stress, and Fear into Vibrance, Strength, and Love.* New York: Harmony Books, 2004.

Pert, Candace. *Molecules of Emotion.* New York: Touchstone, 1999.

Ray, Paul H., and Sherry Ruth Anderson. *The Cultural Creatives: How 50 Million People Are Changing the World.* New York: Harmony Books, 2000.

Rilke, Rainer Maria. *Letters to a Young Poet.* Translated by M. D. Herter Norton. New York: W. W. Norton, 1954.

Rumi. *The Essential Rumi.* Translated by Coleman Barks. San Francisco: HarperSan Francisco, 1995.

Spence, Gerry. *The Making of a Country Lawyer: An Autobiography.* New York: St. Martin's Press, 1996.

Starhawk. *Dreaming the Dark: Magic, Sex, and Politics.* Boston: Beacon Press, 1982.

Stevens, José. *The Power Path: The Shaman's Way to Success in Business and Life.* Novato, CA: New World Library, 2002.

Villoldo, Alberto. *The Four Insights: Wisdom, Power, and Grace of the Earthkeepers.* Carlsbad, CA: Hay House, 2006.

Virtue, Doreen. *Chakra Clearing.* CD. Carlsbad, CA: Hay House, 1997.

Williams, Margery. *The Velveteen Rabbit, or How Toys Become Real.* New York: Smithmark Publishers, 1995.

Whyte, David. *River Flow: New & Selected Poems 1984–2007.* Langley, WA: Many Rivers Press, 2007.

Index

Accepting yourself, 142
Accidental heroes, 15–16
Acting, speaking as, 12
Affirmations and energy, 141
Alchemy of change, 143–152
Alice in Wonderland (Carroll), 153
Altomare, Mary, 146–147, 148
American Women in Communi-
    cation, 36
Amoeba model of change, 146–147
Anderson, Sherry, 86
Angel Therapy (Virtue), 114
Anger. *See also* Outrage
    and change, 19–20
    and home zone, 47
Anxiety. *See* Fear
Archangels, 139
Aron, Elaine, 22
Arrien, Angeles, 18, 41, 70, 164,
    187–188
    on questions and answers, 97
    and quotations, 99
Art of Convening training, 108
Art of speaking, 5
AtKisson, Alan, 147
Attitude, 43–44
Attraction, law of, 19
Audience
    consideration of, 80–84

expectations of, 12–13
eye contact with, 117
handouts to, 177–178
and home zone, 46
intimacy, creating, 103–104
prejudging, mistake of, 84–85
presentations involving, 94–95
researching nature of, 83–84
for rough draft rehearsal, 105
and thinking styles, 86–87
and wisdom of the room, 94–95
Authentic power, 19–20

Bainbridge Graduate Institute, 125
Barks, Coleman, 54–55
Bells, Stevi, 140
Benson, Robyn, 92
Berg, Lisa, 87–88
Berman, Tzeporah, 53–54, 158
Better story
    leaving audience with, 94
    telling, 153–165
*Beyond Survival, A POW's Inspiring
    Story* (Coffee), 42–44
Blessed Unrest (Hawken), 3, 162
Bless You, Mom (West), 79
Body, paying attention to, 121–128
Bombed speeches, 25–27
Born, Paul, 143

Bossin, Bob, 53–54
Bouius, Runa, 125
Brady, Tom, 159
Breast cancer, 131–133
Breathing exercises, 114–116
Brem, Joanne, 32–33
Brow chakra, 138
Brown, Juanita, 108
Buddha, 78, 146

Call to hero's quest, 51
Campbell, Joseph, 15, 42, 50. *See also*
    Hero's journey
Carbonconcierge.com, 125
Casket communiqué, 59–60, 79
Castle, Victoria, 161
Casual venues, 108
Celebrity speakers, 9–10
Centering yourself, 135–137
Centers for Disease Control and
    prevention (CDC), 123–124
Chakra clearing, 137–138
Chakra Clearing (Virtue), 114, 138
Challenge of journey, 51
Chaloult, Pam, 26
Change
    agents of, 1–3
    alchemy of, 143–152
    amoeba model of, 146–147
    anger and, 19–20
    invitation to change, 96
    resonance to, 148–149
    social change and outrage, 19–20
    world change principle, 16–18
Chapman, Jennifer, 70–71
Child voice tone, using, 70–71
Circle technology, 108
Clearwater, Elizabeth, 92
Coaching, 13–14
    in-the-moment, 95–96
Coffee, Jerry, 42–44
Comfort zone, 28, 45–46
Commas, verbal, 70
Community, experience of, 143–144
Compassion and stories, 41
Computer-generated visuals, 13

Conference staging, 109–119
Control, myths about, 11–12
Cook, Carmen, 144
Core message, 58–60
    commitment to, 82
    one good word as, 79–80
    signature statement emphasizing,
        93–94
Corporate alchemy, 146–148
Crown chakra, 138
The Cultural Creatives (Ray & Ander-
    son), 86
Cultural creatives (CCs), 86

Dalai Lama, 155
Daly, Tyne, 149
Dancing with the Tiger (Nattrass &
    Altomare), 146–147
Deadpan humor, 99
Dead space, eliminating, 108–110
De Klerk, F. W., 155
DeMartini, John, 66, 71
Didion, Joan, 157
Disciplines, 63
    inner selves, enlivening voices of,
        72–77
    tempo, varying, 65–67
    verbal punctuation, 69–72
    voice tone and message, aligning,
        67–69
Dossey, Barbara, 159
Dreaming stories, 55–56
Dylan, Bob, 162

Echo microphones, 111
Elder voice tone, using, 71–72
Ella Baker Center for Human
    Rights, 158
Ellis, Dave, 50, 92
Emofree.com, 141
Emotional Freedom Technique
    (EFT), 141–142
Emotions
    energy and, 140–142
    flatlines, 50
    and home zone, 47–49

strong emotion, 49–50
and true self, 33
vibrations and, 145–146
Empathy
and energy, 21–22
intuitive empaths, 22, 135
Emphasis, using, 69–70
Ending sentences, 65
Energetics of speaking, 5–6
Energy
application of, 20
awareness, 129–142
centering yourself, 135–137
chakra clearing, 137–138
fear, removing, 140
luminous energy field, 53
personal energy, sustaining, 21
power and personal energy,
134–140
sacred space, creating, 139–140
shielding/protection practices,
138–139
in speaking environment, 133–134
Equipment requirements, 111–113
Evaluations, asking for, 178
Exclamation marks, verbal, 70
Experience, claiming, 104
Extroverts, body rules for, 126
Eye contact with audience, 117

Face of content, matching voice tone
to, 70–72
Failed speeches, 25–27
Falling Awake Coaching, 50, 92
False fronts, deconstructing, 33–35
Fast speaking style, 66–67
Fear
breathing exercises and, 114
energy psychology and, 140–141
of great speakers, 10–11
liberation from, 15
Feedback, asking for, 178
Fee schedules, 170–172
in letter of agreement, 173–174
sample fee schedule, 171–172
Feet, awareness of, 136–137

Feigenbaum, Cliff, 159
Fero, Alanna, 70
Filler words, avoiding, 66
Florence Nightingale (Dossey), 159
Flying Lessons (Tracta), 132–133
Follow-up communications, 178
Forché, Carolyn, 131–132, 162–163
Ford, Henry, 12–13
Formulaic speaking, avoiding, 23
The Four-Fold Way (Arrien), 18
The Four Insights (Villoldo), 52
Four Winds Society's Healing the
Luminous Body, 55
The Friendship House, 160
Fritz, Robert, 39
Full presence, 18
Fun and speaking, 64

Galeano, Eduardo, 92
Gandhi, Mahatma, 146, 151, 155
Gathering of Women Entrepreneurs, 26
Giraffe Heroes Project, 42
Gladwell, Malcolm, 147
Glib remarks, 82–83
God Without Religion (Saranam), 114
Goodall, Jane, 112–113
Good news, relaying, 83
Gore, Al, 96, 153–154
Gratitude, 165
Great presentations
better story, leaving audience
with, 94
home zone, opening from, 91–92
humor in, 99–103
inspirational closings, 97
invitation to change in, 96
key points, covering, 93
questions and answers in, 97–98
quotations in, 98–99
signature statements in, 93
signature story in, 92–93
spontaneity, organizing for,
89–90
GreenMoney Journal, 159
Grounding yourself, 135–137

Haji, Priya, 159–160
Handheld microphones, 111
Handouts, 177–178
Harvey, Andrew, 155–156
Harvey, Paul, 9
Hawken, Paul, 3, 162
Hawkins, David, 29, 144–146,
    148–149
Haynes, Janice Becker, 156
Health
    paying attention to, 121–128
    sustaining, 20–22
Heart chakra, 138
Heart of speaking, 5
Hedgebrook, xv
Helplessness, 20
Hero's journey, 15–16
    mining material from, 39–41
    witnessing your, 50–52
Higher voice tones, using, 68
The Highly Sensitive Person (Aron),
    22
Hogan, Pasha, 132
Hollyhock Retreat Centre, 26–27,
    187
    questionnaire about, 167–169
    Spirited Speaking class, 47,
        169–170
Holy Fool archetype, 42
Homecoming from journey, 51
Home zone, 28, 45–60
    emotions and, 47–49
    opening from, 91–92
    and storytelling, 46–49
Hope
    inspirational closing and, 97
    radiation of, 21
Hopi prophecy, 157
Hotels, choosing, 125
How to Argue and Win Every Time
    (Spence), 84
Humanmetrics.com, 126
Humor, 37
    and fast-speaking, 66
    in presentations, 99–103

I Ching or Book of Changes, 6
"Illumination" (Haynes), 156
Illumination level of speaking,
    54–55
Imagination level of speaking, 54
An Inconvenient Truth (Gore), 96
Information level of speaking, 54
Ingerman, Sandra, 17, 188
    on negative thoughts, 135
    travel rules, 125
Inner Bonding (Paul), 150
Inner space, 113–116
Innovation diffusion, 147
Insight level of speaking, 54
Inspirational closings, 97
Institute of Cultural Affairs, 86–87
Instructions, list of, 106–113
In-the-moment coaching, 95–96
Intimacy, creating, 103–104
Introductions
    communications about, 177
    writing, 116–117
Intuitive empaths, 22, 135
Invitation to change, 96
Isaacs, David, 108
Isagenix International, 34–35
"I" terms, using, 104

Jay, Paul, 162
Jesus Christ, 146
Jones, Van, 158
Journey. *See* Hero's journey
Joy, 21, 148–149
Judging Amy, 149–150
Judgmental thoughts, 17–18
Jung, Carl, 126

Kennedy, John F., 94
Keynote Camp, 187
Keynote speakers, fees for, 170
Key points, covering, 93
The Kid, 71
King, Martin Luther, Jr., 94, 155, 158
Kouns, Charles, 160
Krishna, 146

Kucinich, Dennis, 98

Lapel microphones, 111
Large spaces, avoiding, 109
Larson, Gary, 80
La Sha, Kelly, 130–131
Lecterns, 110–111
Legend of the Rainbow Warriors
(McFadden), 165
Letters of agreement, 172–174
client contact information in, 173
details of presentation in, 173
fees and expenses in, 173–174
Life, respect for, 155
Life myths, 159
Light, protecting energy with, 139
Liquid Mirror (La Sha), 130–131
Listening to stories, 41
Little Miss Sunshine, 24–25
Living Heroes Essay Contest, 42–43
"Loaves and Fishes" (Whyte), 78
Logo, choosing, 29, 32
Lotus qigong/meditation, 32
Loving yourself, 142
Lower voice tones, using, 68
Luminous energy field, 53

Macy, Joanna, 164
Madame Ovary, 100
Madonna microphones, 112
Magical thinking, 157
The Making of a Country Lawyer
(Spence), 84–85
Mandela, Nelson, 15, 155
McFadden, Steven, 165
McGee, Dawn, 68
Medlock, Ann, 42
Medvec, Emily, 64
The Meeting Manager, 187
Meeting technology, 108
Meilleur, Roberta, 136–137
Memories, expression of, 79–80
Message. *See also* Core message
tone of voice and message, align-
ing, 67–69

Microphones, 111–112
Millman, Dan, 109–110
Mind Over Mountains, 160–161
Molecules of Emotion (Pert), 140
Moyers, Bill, 15
Multiple exhalations exercise,
115–116
Myers-Briggs personality type, 126
Myths of great speaking, 10–14

Nattrass, Brian, 71, 146–147, 148
Natural talent, speaking as, 11
Nature, reflection on, 17
Neal, Craig, 108
Negative feelings, 17
Neural pathways, 141
Newell, Carol, 154
New stories
developing, 57–58
letting in, 41–42
Nunnally, Cathy, 29

Obama, Barack, 94
Obstacles to journey, overcoming, 51
Old stories, shedding, 55–56
On-site communications, 177–178
Openness to outcome, 18
ORID method, 87
Original medicine, 4–5, 14–15
claiming, 27–29
true self, liberating, 32–35
Orloff, Judith, 21, 135
Outcome, openness to, 18
Outer space, requirements for,
106–113
Outrage
place for, 149–152
and social change, 19–20
Over-sharing by participants, 96

Parlett, Isabel, 168
Passion and empathy, 22
The Path of Least Resistance (Fritz), 39
Paul, Margaret, 150
Pausing in speeches, 65–66

Peale, Norman Vincent, 129
Peck, Scott, 16
Perception
    and public speaking, 54–55
    revealing framework of, 52–54
Perls, Fritz, 11, 114
Personal well-being, sustaining,
    20–22
Perspectives and ORID method, 87
Pert, Candace, 140–141
Physical health, sustaining, 20–22
Planning, 36
Podiums, 110–111
Positive Energy (Orloff), 21
Possibilities, elevating, 57–58
Power
    authentic power, 19–20
    choosing, 143–152
    of higher values, 20
    personal energy and, 134–140
    from within, 149
The Power of Positive Thinking (Peale),
    129
The Power Path (Stevens), 139
PowerPoint presentations, 112–113
Power vs. Force (Hawkins), 29,
    144–146
Prayer, 114
    sacred space, creating, 139
Prearrival questionnaire, 173–176
Precious, Russell, 115, 161–162
Preferred voice, using, 73
Principles of transformational
    speaking, 14–22
Proctor, Barbara Gardner, 91
Professional endeavors, mining, 29,
    32
Programs
    order, determining, 107
    sample descriptions, 169–170
Protecting energy, 138–139
Psychological contracts with audi-
    ence, 82

Quadratos (Shaia), 56
Qualities of great speaker, 30–31

Questions and questionnaires
    evaluations, asking for, 178
    in great presentations, 97–98
    Hollyhock Retreat Centre ques-
        tionnaire, 167–169
    prearrival questionnaire, 173–176
    on rehearsing, 105
Quotations, using, 98–99

Ray, Paul, 86
Real Speaking, 1–2, 169–170, 187
Referrals, 178
Rehearsed speakers, 3
Rehearsing rough drafts, 104–105
Relationships, 127–128
Reliving stories, 47–49
A Return to Love (Williamson), 15
Reynolds, Kim, 160–161
Rilke, Reiner Maria, 44, 79
The Road Less Traveled (Peck), 16
Robbins, Tony, 26
Rogers, Everett M., 147
Room, wisdom of the, 94–95
Roosevelt, Eleanor, 98
Root chakra, 137
Roper Green Gauge study on
    change, 148
Roppel, Chuck, 34
Rosenthal, Marc, 84
Rough drafts, rehearsing, 104–105
Rude magnificence, 72–73
Rumi, 54–55, 57, 73, 133, 157, 162

Sacral chakra, 137
Sacred activism, 155
Sacred space, creating, 139–140
Saint-Exupéry, Antoine de, 104
Saranam, Sankara, 114–115
Scheherazade, story of, 151
The Second Half of Life (Arrien), 164
The Secret (DeMartini), 66, 129–130
Self-care, 124
    sustaining, 20–22
Sentences
    emphasis, using, 69–70
    ending, 65

Shadow, nature of, 17
Shaia, Alexander, 56
Shamans, 53
  and sacred space symbols,
    139–140
Shaw, George Bernard, 98
Shielding energy, 138–139
Signature statements, 93
Signature story, 38–39
  in great presentations, 92–93
Silkwood, Karen, 85
Simon, Tami, 26
Sipping circles, 29, 32
"The Skinny on Liposuction" (Larsen), 100–102
Slide projectors, 112–113
Slowing down speaking, 66
Slow speaking style, 67
Social change and outrage, 19–20
Social Venture Network (SVN), 26
  carbonconcierge.com, 125
Solar plexus chakra, 137
Solomon, Joel, 154
Solomon, Linda, 35, 48
Soul, addressing symptoms of, 53
Southard, Kate, 36–38
Space
  inner space, requirements for,
    113–116
  outer space, requirements for,
    106–113
Speaking environment
  control of, 11–12
  energy in, 133–134
Specific information, using, 103–104
Spence, Gerry, 84–85
Spirited Speaking, 47, 169–170
Spontaneity, 89–90
Square breathing exercise, 115
Staging of conference, 109–119
Standing microphones, 111–112
Starhawk, 143–144
Stein, Gertrude, 25, 39
Steinem, Gloria, 4
Stelter-Brolly, Janine, 34–35
Stevens, José, 139, 157, 158, 188

Stevens, Lena, 188
Stewart, Nicole Sedgwick, 103
Storyboards, 90
Story Power: Speak Out to Stand
    Out, 26, 36
Storytelling. *See also* New stories
  better story, telling, 153–165
  dreaming stories, 55–56
  emotion, place for, 49–50
  from hero's journey, 39–41
  home zone, accessing, 46–49
  myths about, 12
  old story, shedding, 55–56
  self-aggrandizement and, 42–44
  signature stories, 38–39
  and true self, 35
Strandberg, Coro, 66, 71
Stress
  health problems and, 123–124
  management of, 21
Strong emotion, place for, 49–50
"Sulphur Passage" (Bossin), 53–54
"Sweet Darkness" (Whyte), 74
Symbols and sacred space, 139–140

"Talk About Speakers" (Larsen), 187
Tamarack Institute, 143
Tears. *See* Emotions
Tempo of speech
  varying, 65–67
  voice tone and, 71
Tension relaxation exercise, 115
Thank-you notes, 178
Thinking styles, 86–87
Third-eye chakra, 138
Thoughts, controlling, 17–18
Throat chakra, 138
The Tipping Point (Gladwell), 147
Tone of voice. *See* Voice tone
Tracta, Pam Hale, 132–133
The Trance of Scarcity (Castle), 161
Travel
  airline travel, 125–126
  letters of agreement including
    expenses, 174
  pressures of, 121–123

Trudell, John, 19, 149
True self
    false fronts, deconstructing,
        33–35
    liberating, 32–35
Truth, 18
    unadorned truth, finding, 44
Tutu, Desmond, 155

Understanding, opening avenues
    of, 18
Unknown, journey to, 51
Unnecessary, eliminating, 104

Valley Girl syndrome, 68–69
The Velveteen Rabbit (Williams), 163
Venues
    energy fields of, 133–134
    requirements for, 107–111
Vibrations and emotions, 145–146
Victimization, sense of, 20
Videos with speech, 112–113
Villoldo, Alberto, 52–53, 55, 138, 188
Virtue, Doreen, 114, 138, 139, 188
Visual equipment, 112–113
Voice tone
    and audience, 81–82
    face of content, matching, 70–72
    inner self, using voices of, 72–77
    list of voices, 75–76
    message, alignment with, 67–69
Volunteers
    from audience, 95
    in-the-moment coaching of,
        95–96

Water during speech, 111, 126
Watson, Lynn, 84
Way of the Peaceful Warrior (Millman),
    109
"The Well of Grief" (Whyte), 40,
    157–158
Wesselman, Hank, 188
West, Harmony, 79–80
"We" terms, using, 104
What the Bleep Do We Know?, 141
Whyte, David, 34
    "Loaves and Fishes," 78
    "Sweet Darkness," 74
    "The Well of Grief," 40, 157–158
Williamson, Marianne, 15
Wireless microphones, 111
Wisdom of the room, 94–95
Wondergem, Casey, 91
World Café process, 108
World change principle, 16–18
World Dance, 136–137
World of Good, 159–160

Yacoboni, Celeste, 29, 32
The Year of Magical Thinking
    (Didion), 157

Zia Pueblo Indians, 29
Ziglar, Zig, 96
Zingarelli, Vito, 47

About the Author

Gail Larsen is a communications coach, speaker, workshop leader, group facilitator, and originator of transformational events. In 1991, she founded Real Speaking (formerly Keynote Camp). In addition to her programs on Whidbey Island, Washington, and in Santa Fe, New Mexico, Gail teaches at Hollyhock Retreat Centre on Cortes Island in British Columbia, Hollyhock Leadership Institute in Vancouver, Royal Roads University in Victoria, and Omega Institute in Rhineback, New York.

A former executive vice president of the worldwide National Speakers Association, Gail has been instrumental in the success of numerous prominent speakers. For four years, her monthly column "Talk About Speakers" appeared in Meeting Professionals International's publication *The Meeting Manager.*

From 1992 to 2002, Gail studied with cultural anthropologist Angeles Arrien to apply cross-cultural wisdom to contemporary life, team building, and conflict resolution. She received her facilitation training at the Institute for Cultural Affairs in Phoenix, Arizona. In addition to ongoing study of shamanism with José and Lena Stevens, Sandra Ingerman, Hank Wesselman, and Alberto Villoldo, she has also been certified with Doreen Virtue, PhD, to expand her capacity to access intuitive and spiritual guidance and support others in this process.

Gail would love to hear from you! Visit www.transformational speaking.com or email Gail at gail@realspeaking.net.

To receive the occasional Real Speaking Power Points e-letter, learn more about the Real Speaking training, engage Gail to speak at your conference, or discuss a program especially designed for your company, organization, or board of directors, please visit www.realspeaking.net or call 1-360-730-1707.

Permissions